Other books by Arnold Palmer

GO FOR BROKE
SITUATION GOLF
MY GAME AND YOURS

ARNOLD PALMER'S BEST 54 GOLF HOLES

Arnold Palmer's
BEST 54 GOLF HOLES

by Arnold Palmer

with Bob Drum

PHOTOS BY ERNEST BAXTER
DIAGRAMS BY JIM C. JOHNSON

Doubleday & Company, Inc., Garden City, New York
1977

Library of Congress Cataloging in Publication Data

Palmer, Arnold, 1929–
  Arnold Palmer's best 54 golf holes.

  1. Palmer, Arnold, 1929–   2. Golf
3. Golf-links–United States.   I. Drum, Bob.
II. Title.
GV964.P3A287   796.352'092'4 [B]
ISBN: 0-385-05259-6
LIBRARY OF CONGRESS CATALOG CARD NUMBER 74–18822

Contents

PAR-FIVES

★ Indicates Arnie's "Best 18"

Introduction

I know, and I'm sure you do, too, that picking the best holes in America is a matter of individual choice.

When we first came up with the idea of the television show that was the father of this book, I thought we would take forever to decide on what to do. I started thinking about all the golf courses I have played. To narrow it down to eighteen holes seemed impossible.

Yet, in the long run, it is individualistic. These are mine. I'm sure that everybody else tackling the same job would have a different list. I would bet that a thousand golf-knowledgeable people would never come up with a single matching eighteen holes.

The reason I have chosen two holes at Augusta National Golf Club is that they are two of the most important ones on a great course that changed my whole way of life. A new era began for me is 1958 when I won my first of four Masters in seven years. This is my bow to Augusta National.

Surely, I could have gone on picking holes forever and a day and not satisfy anybody. In fact, there were so many fine holes and courses that we expanded Arnold Palmer's "best eighteen" to fifty-four holes in this book.

And it was fun. It was fun reliving my life as we filmed the holes. It brought to mind instances almost too numerous to mention. It was enjoyable, too, meeting with old friends at these sites, not in competition, but just having fun for the day under the camera's eye.

Lee Trevino at Baltusrol, where it all began for him. Ben Crenshaw, who should be playing championship golf for the next twenty years. Laura Baugh, perhaps the prettiest golfer I have ever seen.

And then my father, the Deacon. I couldn't have been prouder when Pap made his birdie in front of the cameras.

When you consider I have been playing and competing in golf tournaments for more than thirty years, we could have picked the most interesting three hundred holes, or five hundred holes. It was an endless job. Each time I thought of one hole, another came to mind.

Some famous holes are missing, but this should not be considered rejection. In some cases, I tried to pick holes that were as good, and not quite so famous. Even at that, many of the choices were the consensus of my staff, myself, and many of my player friends on the tour.

Let me emphasize that I am not contending that the fifty-four holes in this book are the "greatest" in America. I don't feel that label of "greatness" is within my grasp. These are, instead, fifty-four interesting or exceptional holes that I have played, with just a few exceptions, at fifty-three different golf courses throughout the country. In many cases, it was something that happened to me or to the world of golf that led me to a particular hole or course. I hope that you appreciate and enjoy this subjectivity.

I had a lot of help with this book, and I want to thank Bob Drum, who has shared many of my greatest experiences for thirty years, for his writing assistance; my personal associate, Doc Giffin, who worked with us in preparing the finished manuscript; and our many friends in golf who were our informal consultants in selecting and describing these holes.

Best of all, I want to thank you, the golf fans. Without you, I would be a lonely man. You have made it all possible.

Arnold Palmer

ARNOLD PALMER'S BEST 54 GOLF HOLES

Par Fours

In selecting the par-fours for this book, I kept one thing in mind—that most great golf courses have strong par-fours, the backbone of the eighteen-hole stretch.

Because there are more par-fours than par-threes and par-fives, I had more chances to come up with good holes.

As I played these holes once again while searching for words for the book, I couldn't help but think that the par-four hole is sort of the orphan of golf.

Spectacular eagles are made at par-fives, and the hole-in-one is only possible at a par-three (those I have played, at least).

Alas, the par-four is subjected to a rare eagle on a holed iron shot. Let us go and visit this stepson of the links, who is known more for his bogeys than his eagles.

The Country Club

BROOKLINE, MASSACHUSETTS

COMPOSITE COURSE,
11th HOLE, 445 YARDS, PAR 4

The Country Club at Brookline, Massachusetts, dates back into the nineteenth century—to a six-hole course built in 1892.

The present course, finished in 1910, was the scene of the first breakthrough in tournament golf by an American. In The Country Club's memorable first Open championship in 1913, a young member, Francis Ouimet, tied for first place with Harry Vardon and Ted Ray, two behemoths of the game from across the Atlantic. In the playoff the next day, Ouimet emerged victorious, and American dominance of tournament golf grew from that brilliant start.

On the fiftieth anniversary of Ouimet's victory, the 1963 U. S. Open was again played at The Country Club—it was one of four Opens in a six-year period in which I finished first. Julius Boros, Jacky Cupit, and I tied after seventy-two holes, and Boros won the playoff.

The course was redesignated for the Open championship with holes from the old eighteen and the new nine adapted for play. The eleventh hole I describe here is the eleventh from the Open championship course.

It is a demanding par-four with the green blind from the tee. A slight draw of the tee shot down the tree-lined fairway leaves the player with a long iron or wood shot across the pond guarding the entire front of the

Arnold Palmer chips with Dick Siderowf as caddy looks on.

green. Typical of The Country Club's greens, it is small with a bunker on the right and woods on the left.

A poor tee shot forces a lay-up and a one-putt for a par. In the 1963 Open playoff, I hit a bad tee shot. It bounced into the stump of a tree in the left rough that had been knocked down by lightning. I wound up with a seven, which cost me the championship.

In my return visit to Brookline, I played the hole with Dick Siderowf, the 1973 British Amateur champion and a long-time amateur standout from New England. Dick has won nearly every amateur title going and still has a zest for the game. I asked Siderowf if he had ever considered becoming a professional. He is surely proficient enough.

"I actually turned for a week after I got out of the service. I declared my intention because I was ready to go. But, after thinking it over for a week, I decided I'd do better as an amateur and enjoy the game more. Of course, in those days, first prize for the U. S. Open was something like twenty-five hundred dollars.

"If I were coming out of college now, I would surely turn with all that money being dangled around. I don't regret my decision. Yet, in the winter

4

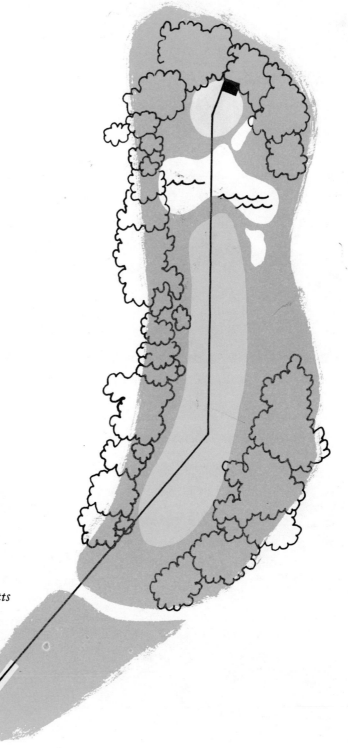

The Country Club
Brookline, Massachusetts
11th Hole, Par 4

Overhead shot of the 11th green (upper right).

View of the green from behind sand trap at golfer's left.

Aerial shot of the hole from behind the tee (fairway to right side).

when the snow is on the ground and I read about Los Angeles, San Diego, Hawaii, I kinda wish I was there.

"But you can't have it all. I spend a lot of time with my wife and children. I know some guys on the tour and they miss that. It's tough on them, too. But you have to do what's best for you, and I'm glad I'm an amateur."

The day we played the eleventh hole, Dick and I both hit good drives to the left side of the fairway, exactly where you want to position your tee shot. Dick hit a two-iron shot that cleared the pond but well to the right of the hole on the fringe. I hit a four-iron that crossed the water but stopped short of the green.

Siderowf chipped past about five feet, and I then chipped in for a birdie three. Dick made his par. Walking off the green, I couldn't help but think what that three would have meant ten years before. It would have saved me four shots on the one hole.

Our low handicapper, who is not in the class of the British Amateur champion but a good player, will have trouble on this hole. If you get in the rough, you can't go for the green, and our low handicapper will put his tee shot either in the rough or the right side of the fairway nine times out of ten. So he will have to lay up short of the pond and try to wedge it close for a par.

7

Our middle handicapper cannot reach the green in two shots, so it is actually a par-five for him. Two wood shots get him to where he can hit a wedge or nine-iron to the green. Then it's one putt for four or two putts for five.

Our high man gets something of a break here. Even if he hits the ball poorly, three shots get him down near the pond for a go at the green. The way he hits his fourth shot will determine his score. He should be able to get over the pond in four and two-putt for a six.

It was thrilling to come back to The Country Club, bringing back some memories for me, although not particularly pleasant ones of the tournament.

I caught a touch of dysentery the night before the playoff and was up all night. The remedy—a jolt of blackberry brandy—left me a bit woozy. I don't mean that as an excuse. I probably would have lost anyway.

Jacky Cupit is the one who has to have nightmares when he thinks of Brookline. He doubled-bogeyed the seventy-first hole to dissipate a two-shot lead. Then he played a marvelous shot to the eighteenth green about ten feet below the cup. I had just made a putt from there for my par. Jacky was going for the whole ball of wax but missed.

The next day, Boros took care of us with a seventy. Cupit shot a seventy-three, and I had a seventy-six. Jacky never came so close to a major title before or since.

Southern Hills Country Club

TULSA, OKLAHOMA

12th HOLE, 456 YARDS, PAR 4

Southern Hills Country Club in Tulsa, Oklahoma, is the premier golf course in the southwestern section of our country, having hosted our three major championships—the 1958 U. S. Open, the 1970 PGA championship, and the 1965 U. S. Amateur—and produced three brand-new major tournament winners. Tommy Bolt came out of the pack to win the Open; Dave Stockton bested me in a head-to-head duel to take the PGA, and Bob Murphy captured the Amateur championship there.

I finished two shots behind Stockton in the 1970 PGA, and the par-four twelfth played a part in my downfall. In the second round I hit my second shot into weeds at the edge of a hazard short of the green and had to stand knee deep in the water to hit the ball. I was worried not only about making the shot but also about a snake biting me on the foot while I was in the water. (I left my shoes on.) Anyway, I took a six on the hole. In retrospect, how nice a par would have been there that day.

The hole has a dogleg to the left. The tee shot lands on the highest part of the fairway at the turn of the dogleg. It is uphill on the tee shot (not too severe), and downhill to the green.

The green is also guarded by water—front right and side. There is a tree on the left about twenty or thirty yards short of the green. Three bunkers line the left side of the putting surface.

A trap nestles in the left elbow of the dogleg. This forces the player to keep the tee shot to the right and usually means his second shot comes in over the water. Because of the extreme length of the hole, the approach is made with a fairly long iron, so it is imperative that the player stay out of the rough on the right side.

Ben Hogan called this the greatest par-four in the country, even though he used to move the ball from left to right when he was playing well. This hole definitely favors the hook, on both the drive and second shot. A hole made for my game, really.

The hole was the key to Bolt's Open win. He birdied it three of four times to edge Gary Player by one stroke. Funny thing there, too. Bolt moved the ball from left to right. Maybe holes that go left favor players that hit the ball to the right.

Southern Hills is credited with one of the great Tommy Bolt stories, although the locale was actually in San Francisco at the Olympic Club. Bolt had played well the first day, and there was a long story in the paper about him, giving his age as forty-nine instead of thirty-nine.

When he finished the second round, he was very much in contention, and the late Charley Bartlett of the Chicago *Tribune*, who was secretary of the Golf Writers' Association of America, tried to persuade Bolt to come to the press room for an interview. Bolt told him nothing doing. Bartlett was at a loss to know why Bolt had refused to be interviewed and asked him.

"Because they made me an old man in today's paper, Charley, that's why," replied Bolt. "I'm not forty-nine years old."

"Oh," replied Bartlett, "that was a typographical error."

"Typographical error, my foot," screamed Bolt. "It was a perfect four and a perfect nine."

On the day Stockton and I returned to Southern Hills, the weather was perfect. We both hit good drives to the right of the fairway bunker and right in the middle of the fairway.

We both hit five-irons this day as the wind was not a factor. I wound up twenty-five feet from the cup, and Stockton was fifteen. We both holed our putts for birdies, but that is not a good gauge of how tough the hole really is. We just played three perfect shots apiece.

I sure wish I had made that three in the PGA championship instead of that watery six. It would have made a better finish to the championship the last day—and I might have sneaked in the winner. But that's water under the bridge, and I never "if" the ball. It doesn't help.

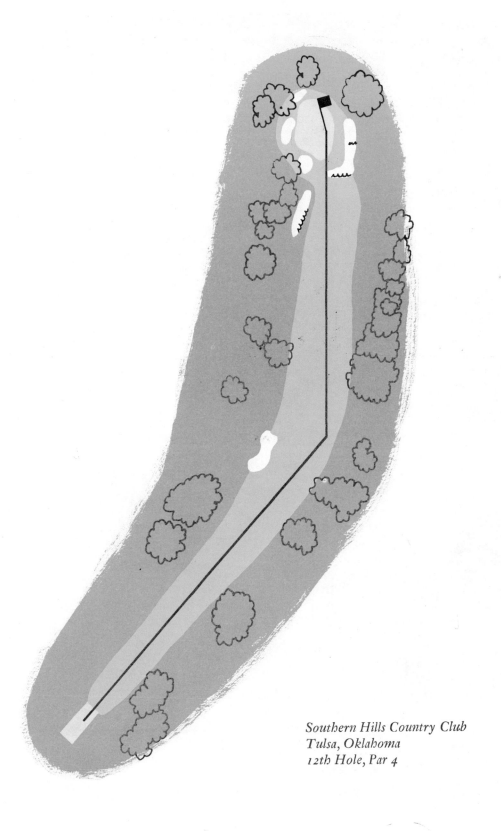

Southern Hills Country Club
Tulsa, Oklahoma
12th Hole, Par 4

Our low handicapper is in the throes of a dilemma on this hole. The fairway bunker comes into play with his tee shot, and the right rough is menacing. He cannot thread the needle all the time, and that's the key to this hole. Perhaps a three-wood tee shot would be best for him, and then either a two-iron or four-wood to the green—that way he would have all the fairway to play with from the tee.

However, knowing our low handicapper, he wants to play with the big boys. Either the sand will get him or the rough eight of ten times. If he gets to the fairway funnel, a four-iron will be sufficient to carry the water and set up a birdie try those other two times. Otherwise, he will have to lay up, play a wedge, and try to one-putt for a par.

Our middle handicapper should be able to make a bogey, which is a good score on this hole. His usual fading tee shot starts toward the left trap and lands on the right side of the fairway. His three-wood second sails over the left fairway trap and lands down near the water short of the green.

Our middle man now is wedge distance from the pin and, depending on how close he gets his shot, he either makes par or a bogey. Not bad, considering he cannot get home in two strokes.

All holes are difficult for our high handicapper, but holes with water slaughter him. On this one he should try to play down the right side of the fairway away from the bunker and should get past it in two or three strokes. Then he should aim his next shot down the left side toward the big tree so he doesn't have to go over water.

Even if he misses a shot, he should be within putting distance of the cup and can two-putt for a seven, which is only one stroke more than it took me to play the hole that one day in the PGA championship.

Dave Stockton blasts from the sand on the second hole in the second round of the 1970 PGA championship at Southern Hills Country Club, Tulsa. (COURTESY WIDE WORLD PHOTOS)

Laurel Valley Golf Club

LIGONIER, PENNSYLVANIA

18th HOLE, 470 YARDS, PAR 4

Laurel Valley has a special meaning to me. It was conceived in the late 1950s by a group of local business executives who have lived in the Ligonier Valley for many years—George Love, Fred Gwinner, George Wyckoff, and Ben Fairless, giants in industry but just plain folks on a golf course.

Laurel Valley is a championship golf course, and it has done all the things the founders wanted it to do. It has hosted the PGA championship and the team championship and was the 1975 venue for the Ryder Cup matches.

The eighteenth at Laurel Valley has particular significance for me. It was there that my good friend Dave Marr won the PGA championship by mustering a par-four under the most difficult circumstances. He was paired with Jack Nicklaus the last day and, on the difficult, par-three seventeenth, Nicklaus chipped in to save a par. Dave then holed a treacherous second putt from eight feet to preserve a two-shot lead going to the final hole.

A two-stroke lead sounds like a lot with just one hole to go, but a birdie for Jack and a bogey for Dave and it's all tied up. The eighteenth at Laurel, at 470 yards, is a particularly tough hole for the average hitter. He not only must be long but also must get the ball in the fairway along the right side to have a chance to have a go at the green.

I remember every shot Dave played on the eighteenth in that final round

14

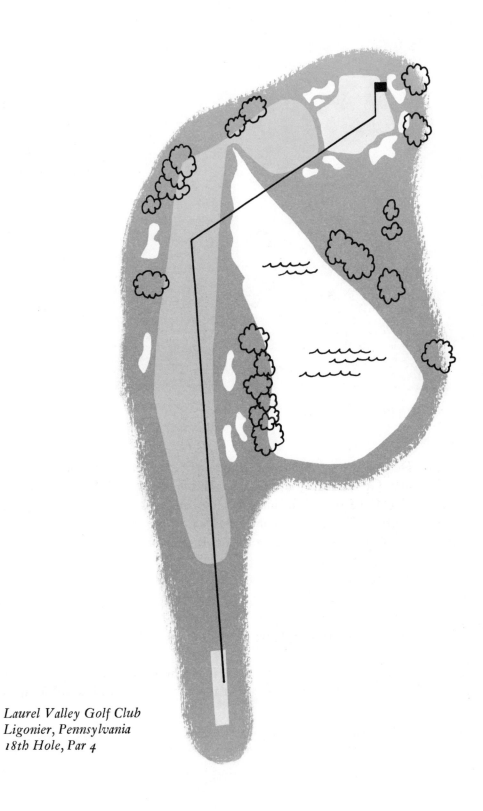

Laurel Valley Golf Club
Ligonier, Pennsylvania
18th Hole, Par 4

Dave Marr hits fairway wood.

in 1965. He pulled his tee shot into the left bunker, and I figured it was all over for him. He then layed up short of the pond and Nicklaus overshot the green, giving Dave some breathing room. Dave took full advantage of the opening, putting his nine-iron shot thirty inches from the hole and knew the title was his. In fact, he told me he started to memorize his "Thank you, everyone" speech after that third shot.

Even for the average professional, the eighteenth at Laurel presents a formidable challenge. The drive must be positioned just right or it becomes a par-five, since there is water at the foot of the slope up to the green. Even with a good drive, nearly everyone must hit a long iron or fairway wood for his second shot.

Bunkers flank both sides of the fairway in the landing area, three on the right side set to catch off-line shots of players attempting to bite off a bit of

Aerial view of Laurel Valley, with 18th shown in upper left section, doglegs at upper end of lake, well-trapped green below clubhouse.

Arnold Palmer hits to green.

the hole's slight dogleg to the right. If the player is bunkered, he has virtually no chance to get his second shot on the green; let's say that the odds are ten to one against him if he chooses to try it.

The second shot must get up in the air because of the green's elevation. If you hit a low shot into the hillside, the ball either stops there in the grass or one of the three traps or drops back into the water. The hole combines the best of two worlds—a fine drive and an exceptional approach.

I asked Dave Marr to come back to play the eighteenth again with me, and he agreed. He said he came back just to make sure it actually was the hole on which he won the PGA championship, since he was in a state of shock at the time and doesn't remember much about it—especially since he had made a double bogey six on it in the third round.

Dave drove straight down the middle of the fairway and had about 230 yards left. He hit a three-wood into a bunker at the right front of the green. I had put my tee shot pretty much in "Position A" and got home with a three-iron, then two-putted for a par. Marr made five from the bunker. He claimed a "half," declaring it was a stroke hole for him.

The green and its protection add measurably to the difficulty of the hole. The green has two tiers and is huge. Besides the three bunkers set into the

The Country Club, Brookline, Massachusetts—11th hole.
View toward fairway from behind flagstick.

Southern Hills Country Club, Tulsa, Oklahoma—12th hole. Aerial view.

Laurel Valley, Ligonier, Pennsylvania—18th hole.
View of green across unusual twin trap at golfer's left.

Oakmont Country Club, Oakmont, Pennsylvania—15th hole. Aerial of massive green.

Cypress Point Club, Pebble Beach, California —17th bole. Scenic view.

Oakland Hills, Birmingham, Michigan — 16th hole. Aerial looking toward green.

Pebble Beach, Pebble Beach, California —8th hole. View looking back from green across elbow of Carmel Bay.

The Champions Golf Club, Houston, Texas—14th hole. View of green across water from golfer's left.

slope in front of the green, three other bunkers fringe the green. It's like hitting over a mirage of water into a high oasis in the Sahara.

Even for a low handicapper, the eighteenth at Laurel is a par-five. There is no room for error on the drive, and an amateur with a four or five handicap tends to be long but wild. He cannot afford that from the back tee of the eighteenth at Laurel.

Even if our low handicapper hits a long drive in the fairway, he must now hit another spectacular shot to the green. He may put the two together on occasions, but the odds are against him. Either the fairway bunkers or the traps around the green will catch him should he make the slightest error.

Figure him to one-putt for pars about three of every ten times he plays the hole. Another thing that lessens the birdie chances is that two-tiered, sloping green. Tough to putt, and when the pin is back, it takes a mammoth second shot just to reach it.

It's a definite par-five for our middle handicapper for the simple reason he cannot reach the green in two shots. His drive will be short of the bunkers, if not in them. His second will have to be short of the water, and his third shot will determine his score. If he gets close, he may one-putt for four. But chances are he will just get on the green somewhere and either two- or three-putt. The green has rolls and swells in it that the inexperienced eye does not detect.

The high handicapper finally has a hole that makes him one of the players —in a way. His first three shots should get him down near the water. Now

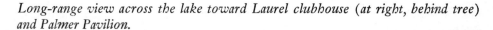

Long-range view across the lake toward Laurel clubhouse (at right, behind tree) and Palmer Pavilion.

the only thing stopping him from making a six (the average score on the hole) is his usual fear of hitting the ball in the water. Our high man should concentrate on hitting the shot and try to forget about the water. In fact, one tip I would like to pass on to you high handicappers of the world (you are in the majority, so don't feel badly) is to concentrate on the back half of the ball as you swing at it. This item of concentration can take as many as ten strokes per round off your score.

Since Laurel Valley is in my backyard, it is easy for me to say nice things about it. When you have so many leaders of business and industry and such a concentration of wealth as we have in the Ligonier Valley, you know it has to be a good place to live.

People ask me why I still live in Latrobe, which is only a few miles from Ligonier and Laurel Valley. I was born there, it is my home, and they are my people. I like the folks in Ligonier, too. Latrobe is a mill town and the people are just great—good, hard-working people who appreciate a good time. To many of them, I'm sure, I'm just a loafer who doesn't know how to do a good day's work. And there's no sense of me arguing with them that golf is hard work. They do five days in the mill so they can afford to play golf, something that made me a mighty fine living. You try to argue that.

Editor's Note

Arnie conveniently has forgotten to mention that the members of Laurel Valley Golf Club think so much of him that he is virtually enshrined there. A new, glass-fronted building overlooking the tenth tee and eighteenth green and the rest of the course and valley beyond them is called the Palmer Pavilion. A tribute to their tournament professional and honorary life member—the boy from Latrobe who rose from the ranks to become a household name in the world of sports.

Oakmont Country Club

OAKMONT, PENNSYLVANIA

15th HOLE, 453 YARDS, PAR 4

Oakmont Country Club has held its head high through most of the twentieth century, and rightly so. Oakmont's famous golf course was built in 1903 by W. C. Fownes and since then has hosted more national championships than any other course in the United States. It weathered well the golfing assaults of the world's greatest players through those seventy years until Johnny Miller came along and gave it a sound trouncing in the 1973 National Open there.

Miller shot an incredible sixty-three on the final day, the lowest round ever shot not only at Oakmont but also in any U. S. Open in history, to capture the championship in its fifth staging at the course in my western Pennsylvania neck of the woods. It takes nothing from Johnny's remarkable finish, but, in fairness to Oakmont's reputation, it should be noted that unusually heavy spring rains had stripped the course of its main armor—lightning-fast greens that usually conquer instead of being conquered.

The subtleties of Oakmont are many. It has few trees in play and no water holes at all, the closest thing being a few drainage ditches. But there are bunkers, untold bunkers that have varied in numbers through the years. In some places, there is so much sand that the golfer would think he is serving in the French Foreign Legion.

21

In earlier years, when Emil Loeffler was the course superintendent, the bunkers were furrowed with a rake that was weighted down with a hundred-pound slab of steel. This produced three-inch furrows with one-inch separations in all the bunkers. Woe befell the player who tried to hit any kind of distance shot from the sand. It invariably failed. The United States Golf Association forced Oakmont to keep the monster rake out of the fairway bunkers during the 1953 Open. Then, in 1962, it became a museum piece, deactivated because modern-day players do not consider furrowed traps a proper hazard in today's game.

During the five National Opens, four U. S. Amateur championships, and two PGA championships at Oakmont, no hole was more decisive in determining the winner than the 453-yard, par-four fifteenth. Ben Hogan described the hole as "the most demanding he had ever played." It is also a hole that has diminished somewhat in difficulty through the years, and nothing could be done to prevent it. The modern equipment and skill of the players have given them greater length, but the fifteenth is already stretched to its limit on the available terrain. The tee lies between the fourteenth green and the eighteenth fairway and would interfere with play of both holes if it were moved back. The big bunkers to the right and left in what was the landing area for the tee shots of the best players no longer constitute the hazards they were in the past. Yet so great is this hole that, even though stripped of some of its majesty from the tee-shot standpoint, it still gives no ground to the players.

The green is out of sight from the tee, but the experienced golfer knows that he wants to put his drive into the left center of the fairway, since the fairway slopes markedly to the right toward a gaping bunker and a drainage ditch awaiting errant shots. Even after a properly placed tee shot, the player faces an awesome challenge.

The green is enormous, even though its original size has been reduced by a third. Once a hundred yards deep, it now measures some sixty-five yards from front to back. The apron and the first fifteen or twenty yards of putting surface slope away from the player. Then the green rises toward the back, gradually leveling off. This creates a valley across the front half of the green. When the pin is cut toward the front, it demands either a skillful pitch-and-run or a perfectly placed iron shot (usually with a middle iron) to stop short of the upslope. Putting from the back of the green is almost a "gimme" three-putt.

Adding to the difficulty of the hole are the bunkers—a long one to the left rear of the green, two to the left in front of the green, and a fifteen-foot-wide, ninety-five-yard-long abyss that starts well out in front of the right side of the green, from which the terrain drops abruptly into the woods. A

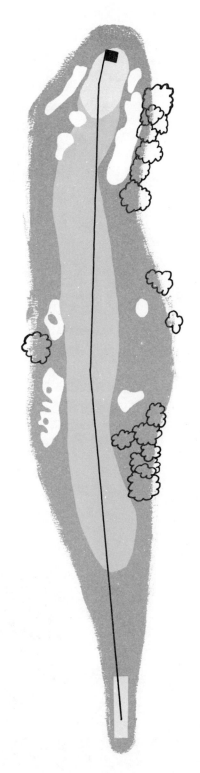

Oakmont Country Club
Oakmont, Pennsylvania
15th Hole, Par 4

player approaching from the right side of the fairway or rough to a pin placement to the right front of the green has one of the toughest shots in golf with the carry over all of that sand, particularly if he has to get close enough for a putt at a birdie. Any fade will put the ball in the right bunker or the trees, while a hooked or pulled approach will leave either a nasty chip shot or shovel bunker shot from sand ten feet below the level of the putting surface.

Putting on the fifteenth is a job for a master surgeon. It is next to impossible to stop the ball in front of the pin unless the pin is on the upper slope, so just about every putt is downhill. If the pin placement is at the back of the green, going for the pin is dangerous because of a fifteen-foot drop behind the green between there and the elevated sixteenth tee. Therefore, most players come up short and have to guess how hard to hit the putt to get up the hill and how much break will occur. They are also conscious of not wanting to run it beyond the hole and then facing a downhill putt coming back.

A low-handicap player (scratch to five) is hard pressed to make par on the fifteenth at Oakmont. Even the most skilled amateur has trouble hitting long tee shots at a small target (in fact, so do most professionals), and from this tee he will try to bust it over the hill so he will be in position to attack the green.

More often than not, he will either let it out to the right and into the rough or bunker, or hook it either into the fairway bunker on the left or beyond it into a small clump of trees near the eighteenth tee, some two hundred yards from the green.

If our low handicapper has a good lie in the right rough, he has a makable shot with a midiron, but he must hit his shot over that monstrous bunker that guards the entire right side of the green. The tendency is to hit it left, trying to avoid a disastrous fade, which means instant bogey. If the lie is bad, he must try to hit a short iron (seven to wedge) somewhere in the fairway short of the green and rely on his chipping and putting for a par, a nearly impossible task.

If he has hit it into the trouble down the left side, he is in bogey town, especially if the pin is from center on to the right. A midiron will either stop short of the green or, if the land is dry, bounce all the way to the back of the green. It is not uncommon for a player to putt down that hill and right off the putting surface.

A good tee shot leaves him a five- or six-iron to the green. Club selection

Aerial view of 15th hole from behind green.

Arnold Palmer practices putting on huge green in front of clubhouse.

is of utmost importance. He wants to stay on the lower level, so he must hit a shot that will carry to the green with bite, unless he employs the pitch-and-run, a shot that is not too familiar to today's players. The pitch-and-run is calculated to land short of the green and bounce to the pin.

The medium (seven to fifteen) handicapper will probably play from the member tees, which, in this case, does not give him much of an edge. He is still faced with hitting the ball slightly uphill and straight and, if he could do either with consistency, he would not be a medium handicapper. As a result, his best bet is to hit a three- or four-wood from the tee, which will leave him short of the big trouble, although he will still have a blind second shot and no chance to get close to the green. His second shot is either a four- or five-wood, or perhaps a four-iron, depending on which feels most comfortable to him. He is now within 150 yards of the putting surface and, if he is as proficient as most medium handicappers whose long suit is short irons, chipping, and putting, the worst score facing him is a bogey.

Of course, we have this golfer playing the course carefully and properly, with little chance for error on his first two shots, which have traversed little more than three hundred yards. Still, if he plays within himself, par is a possibility. Since he has a stroke on the hole, even a bogey will put him in fair shape.

Our high handicapper is in trouble here, but isn't he always? It will take him at least two strokes to get to the top of the hill, unless he hits an unusual (for him) tee shot. The second shot lands in the trouble area, at the narrowest part of the hill, with bunkers on both sides. If, like most high handicappers, he favors the slice, that big bunker on the right is in for a landscaping.

However, if the handicapper wants to make a decent showing (few of them do), he will hit a driver off the tee and, depending on where it lands, must make a decision. If he hits a grounder, the next shot should be with a five-iron, keeping him short of the trouble, then another five-iron beyond it.

If he bloops the ball, the same procedure with the five-iron. If he hits his usual 150-yard slice, the next shot from the rough should be with an eight- or nine-iron to try to get back in play. Whichever shot he hits—the high blooper with or without roll, the grounder that does or doesn't make the fairway, or the big slice that nestles in the rough—he best try to be in the fairway in three. By all means, from anywhere on the right side, hit it to the left.

His trouble is not over yet. If he is where he is supposed to be in this plan of attack, he most likely has a downhill lie, which will cause his slice to slice more, so he should use an iron and get somewhere in the vicinity of the green in four. Assuming that he gets on the green in five, his score is now in the hands of the putter. Surprisingly, some high handicappers are better-than-average putters, since it is the only club that doesn't demand a particularly high degree of skill. Even a child can putt the ball, but few children can swing at it and hit it.

I played the hole recently with Steve Melnyk, who won the 1969 National Amateur championship at Oakmont, and we had considerable success on the hole.

I asked Steve how he played it in the last round of the Amateur championship in 1969.

"Well, it was a lot easier than I thought," Steve said. "I had a seven-shot lead, the wind was behind me, and there was nothing to do but take a big swing. I had no pressure. I really bombed the ball, hit a seven-iron to the green, and made a par-four."

The day Steve and I played the hole, the wind was against us. We both hit good tee shots over the hill. Mine was down the right side of the fairway, and I was away. I hit a two-iron that had a slight hook on it. It went out over the long trap, hit in front of the pin, and rolled right by the hole about six feet. Melnyk hit a four-iron about fifteen feet away, and we both two-putted for pars.

As I left the old course, I couldn't help but think how much golfing history was written there. It was there in 1919 that S. Davidson Herron won the National Amateur by beating the great Bobby Jones in match play.

In 1927, Tommy Armour beat Harry Cooper in a playoff for the Open championship. Then, in 1935, a local professional, Sam Parks, made history by winning the Open with one of the highest scores in the modern game—a 299. He was the only man to break 300. Ben Hogan won his record-tying fourth Open at Oakmont in 1953.

Steve Melnyk tees off.

Low-level aerial from over fairway toward green.

In 1962 Jack Nicklaus won his first tournament as a professional there, and I remember that one well. He beat me in a playoff for the Open title, 71–74, and has gone on to become one of the golfing greats with a vesture in Oakmont's history.

In 1973, I was among the four leaders going into the final round and was playing well the last day. But Johnny Miller came along and scored that incredible sixty-three. I was tied for the lead until I missed a short putt at eleven and eventually finished fourth.

But that's what makes it a great game. And a hole such as the fifteenth at Oakmont that plays so many different ways adds to the joy of the game—or, in many cases, sends its challengers to the sixteenth tee muttering to themselves.

Cypress Point Club

PEBBLE BEACH, CALIFORNIA

17th HOLE, 371 YARDS, PAR 4

The Monterey Peninsula is golf. It's a year-'round thing there, and the weather plays a big part in the action. It's a rare day when the wind doesn't blow strongly and make some of the most difficult holes in the world even more difficult.

Choosing holes on the Peninsula is tough because there are so many good ones there. Just about everybody must know about Cypress Point's famed sixteenth hole, where a finger of the Pacific Ocean churns between the tee and the green of this rugged par-three. Less known, but equally testing, is the seventeenth.

The wind usually sides with the seventeenth and against the player. It blows straight into the golfer's face and makes driving a monumental task. Cypress Point is one of three courses played in the Bing Crosby tournament. In one of those Crosbys—mind you, the hole is only 371 yards long—I hit a driver and a three-iron and was short of the green. The configuration of the holes forces you to drive into the side of a hill when the wind is against you and then carry a big cypress tree to get to the green.

My old friend, Phil Harris, talks about the seventeenth.

"I'm going to tell you one thing that goes back a few years, Arnie, and I

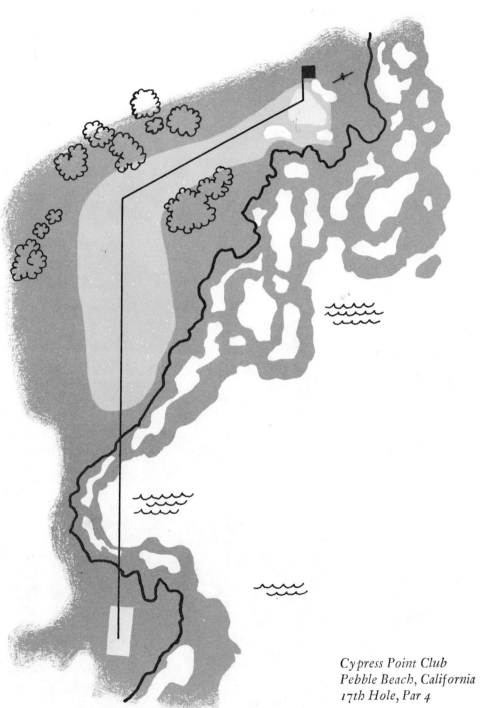

Cypress Point Club
Pebble Beach, California
17th Hole, Par 4

*Aerial view of
green and ocean.*

View of hole from back tee.

think you remember. The elements have a great deal to do with this hole and all the courses on the beach.

"It can hail, it can snow, and I've seen the wind so strong that you couldn't put the ball on a tee. This happened to me one time when I was playing with Cary Middlecoff and Ed Crowley, so help me. We had to quit playing another time because hail was beating a tattoo all over us."

Phil is not exaggerating. I was there in weather like that. I remember another time when Dow Finsterwald hit a shot about three feet from the hole. As he was walking up to mark it, the wind blew it right off the front of the green.

I've had all kinds of things happen to me at Monterey. I was even disqualified once at another seventeenth hole there—the seventeenth at Pebble Beach—because I slipped up on one of the rules of golf. I hit my tee shot down onto the beach, thought it might be on its way out to sea, and hit a "provisional" ball. I found the first ball on the beach but couldn't try to hit it. I declared it unplayable and finished out the hole with the provisional ball. This isn't permitted, I forgot. I should have gone back to the tee and hit yet another tee shot.

Another year I was down on the same beach, trying to decide whether to play a shot from the water, which kept moving the ball around among the rocks. Jimmy Demaret was the television commentator that year, and he was explaining to the TV audience what options I had if I decided to declare the ball unplayable. One, he said, was that I could take a one-stroke penalty and drop my ball behind the spot where it was but keeping it on line with the pin up on the green. "Of course, the nearest dry land for Arnie's drop," Demaret explained, "is Honolulu." (Oh, yes, I played the shot eventually and poorly —and made eight.)

Harris is the father of the "banana ball"—a parabolic dream with its sweeping left-to-right arc. The day we played the seventeenth at Cypress Point, he hit two choice bananas and then used his wedge (he calls it a soup spoon) to drop the ball about six feet past the cup. I used a driver and an eight-iron (there was just a little wind) and two-putted for a par. Phil missed his par putt and happily settled for a five.

To go over the hole again:

The tee shot carries into a fairly spacious fairway but must have good length since the hole doglegs right toward the water with trees lining both sides of the final stretch of fairway. A short tee shot brings the trees into play and so do tee shots that stray too far to the right or left.

Ground-level view of green.

Phil Harris before teeing off.

The green sits near the edge of the ocean cliff. It has a trap in front, one each to the right and left rear. In calm weather, the shot to the green with a fairly short iron is not too demanding. But the hole is almost totally exposed to the frequent storms and usual winds off Carmel Bay and, in such conditions, becomes virtually a different hole—very challenging.

If our low handicapper hits his tee shot well, he will have little trouble with this hole. He will be out far enough to hit a short iron to the green. In inclement weather, the player's handicap really doesn't matter. The hole is boss.

Phil Harris played the hole as a middle handicapper will. Our middle man will hit his tee shot into the rising fairway and be faced with a blind shot to

36

the green. Since so many middle handicappers tend to hit slices, this terrain is built for his next shot. He could get on the green with that second shot from the fairway, so the hole does have birdie possibilities for him.

The high handicapper gets a sort of break here, too. With two decent shots, he should be near the crest of the hill. He might reach the green from there. It slopes down and away toward the green, and even a "grounder" might bounce and roll onto the putting surface. A par there is not out of the question for our man, who has been struggling throughout the pages of this book.

Membership in the Cypress Point Club is quite exclusive. Even during the Crosby tournament, the clubhouse is open only to members and their guests. Presidents Eisenhower and Kennedy were among the great men of our time who have played at Cypress. It is by far the shortest of the three Crosby courses, measuring only 6,317 yards. On the rare calm days, you can count on most of the low scores being shot at Cypress, but even then either the sixteenth or seventeenth grabs a few players for scores in the double figures.

Yes, golf and the weather are inseparable on the Monterey Peninsula.

Oakland Hills Country Club

BIRMINGHAM, MICHIGAN

16th HOLE, 408 YARDS, PAR 4

Oakland Hills has been the scene of some of the greatest championships of modern times and a fountainhead of tales from the old days. Cyril Walker, who was one of the monumental unknowns to capture the Open championship, won here in 1924. Ralph Guldahl, who for two years was the greatest player in the world, won his first Open here in 1937.

The course, steeped in tradition and championships, was remodeled in 1950 for the 1951 Open championship by Robert Trent Jones. Jones narrowed the fairways so much that Cary Middlecoff remarked: "We had to walk single file off the tees to stay out of the rough."

Jones also added sixty-six bunkers at strategic places in the fairways so that driving the ball was akin to shooting a rifle. Ben Hogan went on to win here—it was the second year after his almost fatal auto collision with a bus—for his third Open title in three years (he didn't play in 1949). This also prompted a remark, this one by Claude Harmon: "If you keep playing like this, Ben, every other player is going to go out and get hit by a bus."

It was, indeed, Hogan's shining hour. Only two men in the field broke par of seventy—Hogan with a sixty-seven and Clayton Haefner with a sixty-nine. Bobby Locke, the famed South African, allowed that "Hogan must be

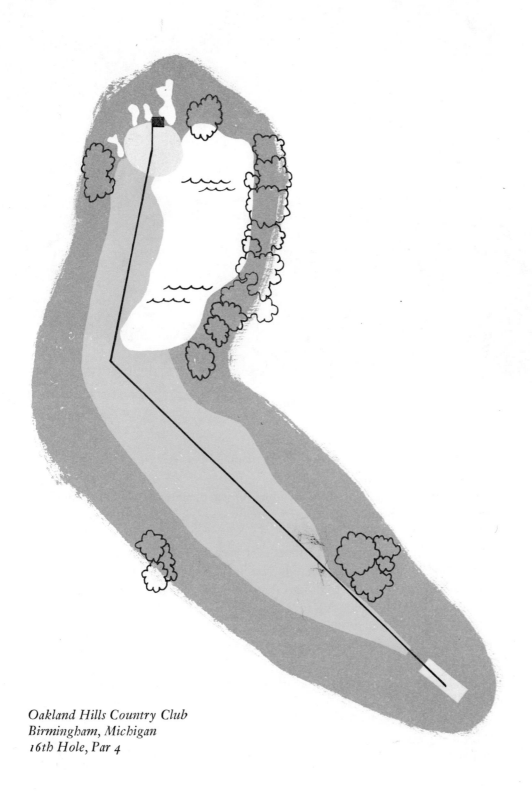

Oakland Hills Country Club
Birmingham, Michigan
16th Hole, Par 4

Scenic view of 16th hole through willows.

playing a different course than the rest of us." I was still in the Coast Guard, but I remember it well.

Then, in 1961, I was the defending Open champion when I arrived at Oakland Hills. I couldn't get started quickly enough as Gene Littler won the title.

One of the greatest pressure shots ever made was by Gary Player in 1972 on Oakland Hills' sixteenth hole. He was in the rough, stymied by a tree, but he played a shot over the tree onto the green, birdied the hole, and went on to win the PGA championship for the second time.

I asked Gary to play the hole again with me, and he kindly accepted the invitation. He was happy to return to the scene of the triumph and explain the shot to me.

"When I arrived at the sixteenth hole in the last round, I had it in my mind that I had been runner-up in five major championships—lost them, actually—and I wanted no more of second. Nobody remembers who finishes second, as you well know. It's happened to you in the Open championship four times.

40

"You see, when we started the final round, there were ten of us all within a stroke of each other, including Sam Snead, of all people. I was stymied by the tree, and the water looked menacing, but I decided that I would go for the win or finish tenth. The way I see it, there is no difference between first and tenth or last. Winning is the only thing.

"I was very lucky. Some lady very kindly left her seat stick right under that tree. I couldn't see the flag but, when I lay on the ground, I could see the flag dead in line with the seat stick. I knew the club to use because the day before I was the same distance away and went at it with a nine-iron.

"So I hit the shot right over the seat stick and ran from behind the tree to watch. It landed three feet from the pin. The tournament was mine from that moment on."

Gary is remarkable. He has traveled so much to play. He lives in South Africa and has to travel halfway around the world just to tee it up. He estimates that in twenty years of competitive golf, he has been away from home about twelve of them.

Player is partly responsible for building up tours in other countries. He will play anywhere there is competition. It's getting to be lucrative to play in Europe, England, and Africa. Japan might even rival the United States in prize money in the near future. Actually, golf is the most international of all sports.

Player is one of only four men in history to have won all four major championships during a career, Jack Nicklaus, Ben Hogan, and Gene Sarazen being the others. I'm short a victory in the PGA championship of joining them.

The day Gary and I played the sixteenth, we both hit good drives, Gary slightly ahead of me. I played a six-iron within twelve feet of the cup. Player put his approach fifteen feet from the hole.

He putted first and made birdie. Then I knocked mine in on top. "I don't think I'll ever play this hole again," Gary commented. "After all, two consecutive threes on one of the great par-fours should suffice."

If I could putt like Gary, I think I would go to South Africa and raise horses, too.

The sixteenth at Oakland Hills is unique in that there is no really safe place to hit your second shot. Water protects almost the entire front and right side of the green and, with the prevailing gusty wind, it is difficult to select the right club for your second shot.

While the hole has a dogleg right around the pond, the dogleg has no bearing on the tee shot. The drive is straightaway, possibly even with a three-wood to keep the ball in the fairway, since the rough on both sides will

*Arnold Palmer
and Gary Player.*

complicate the second shot to the peninsula green; so will those willows to the right that almost put Gary out of action.

The green is trapped to the left, and three bunkers behind the putting surface catch the player who has purposely taken too much club to stay out of the water.

Our low handicapper will be able to play this hole almost the same as a professional. Using a three- or four-wood off the tee, our low man should be able to place the ball in the fairway, which slopes slightly downhill in the landing area. If he selects the right club, our low man should be able to put the ball somewhere on the putting surface for a try at a birdie and a safe par. Only if he hits one of those bunkers behind the green is he in trouble, as the sand shot must be played looking right at the water in front.

Our middle handicapper is in trouble. If he hits a good drive (for him),

Aerial view from behind green.

Low-level view across lake to green.

he still will have 185 or 190 yards to carry over the water to the putting surface. So it is best that he lay up to the left with a short iron and try to wedge
it close for a par. That way, he eliminates the bunkers and the water and,
even if he has to settle for a bogey-five, he has escaped the bugaboo of a
seven or an eight.

Our high handicapper is in trouble again. He's always in trouble when
water protects the green since he has difficulty getting the ball airborne. Our
high man figures to bump the ball two or three times to get to a point from
which he must traverse the water hazard. If he elects to try to cross it, his
score will be determined by how many times he looks up on the shot. (The
major failing of most high handicappers is the inability to keep the head still.
Strike down at the back of the ball with the club and wait until the follow-
through before looking up. The poorer player usually tries to scoop the ball
with the clubhead, which causes him to lift up and mishit the shot most of
the time.)

44

Gary Player has the same great love for golf as I have. I recall what he said that day:

"Golf is such an unusual game. A twenty-four handicapper can play a champion and beat him. There are not many sports in which a sixty-two-year-old man can compete in championships against men who weren't born until he was forty [an obvious reference to Sam Snead].

"Through the years, I have picked up quite a bit of knowledge about golf. So I plan to put a practice range on my ranch. When some of the younger players are having trouble, I could help them with their game. Like your boys' camps.

"Say, you could select two of your best boy players and, as a reward, send them to South Africa to visit me at my ranch. There would be few distractions, and a player could really work on his game."

It sounds so good I may go myself.

Pebble Beach Golf Links

PEBBLE BEACH, CALIFORNIA

8th HOLE, 425 YARDS, PAR 4

The links and Scotland go hand in hand in golf tradition. For many years the British Open was contested only on links, which, oversimplified, are seaside courses. Pebble Beach, on California's Monterey Peninsula, is certainly America's most celebrated seaside course, not only because it is a great test of golf but also because of its tremendous exposure annually on television during the Bing Crosby Pro-Am.

It is spectacularly beautiful the year 'round, with Carmel Bay in the background—seals sunning themselves on the rocks, and sailboats breezing by. It's an artistic wonderland.

This vintage course, opened in 1919, was twice the scene of the U. S. Amateur championship, with Jack Nicklaus winning the second one there in 1961 and turning professional a few months later. Nicklaus returned to Pebble Beach eleven years later and won the U. S. Open, the only time it has been played on the Monterey Peninsula.

Weather is the name of the golf game at Pebble Beach. Rain, hail, even snow once in a great while are winter visitors and, for those not playing in it, the weather shows the vast television gallery one of the big hazards we professional golfers have to face.

I have never won the Crosby, but have been close a few times. Once, in

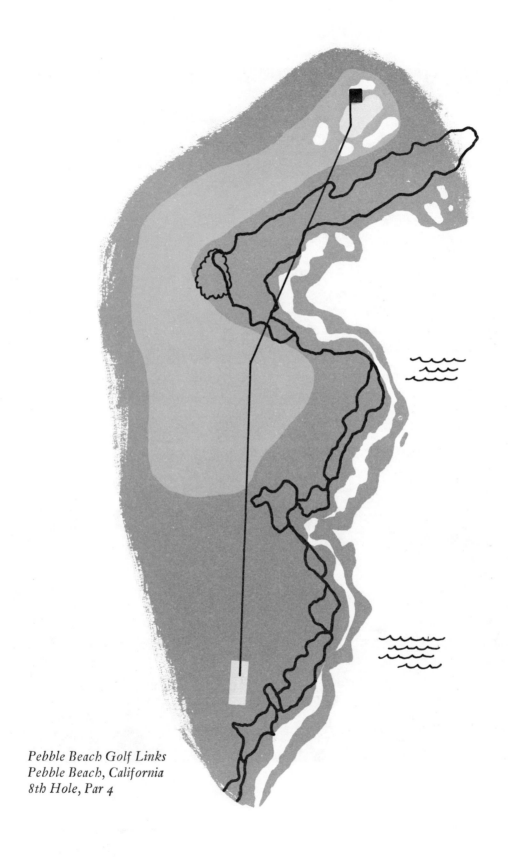

Pebble Beach Golf Links
Pebble Beach, California
8th Hole, Par 4

*Aerial view showing
seventh (foreground)
and eighth (right-
center, starting from
tee on which players
and others appear).*

1967, I was in the thick of things in the final round when I reached the par-five fourteenth hole. Wanting a birdie, I went for the green with my second shot. But that shot and the next one hit the same tree, and both ricocheted out of bounds. A nine on the hole and out. That night a storm hit and knocked down that very tree.

In the Open in 1972, I had a putt at that same hole for a birdie, and Nicklaus, struggling at that point, had a putt at twelve for a par. If I make and he misses, I take the lead. I missed, he made, and he went on to win.

I invited Bob Rosburg to play Pebble Beach's eighth hole with me. I picked that exacting par-four because it is not only a great hole but also because nobody has ever seen it who hasn't walked the course and depends on television for his views of Pebble Beach.

Rosburg is a native northern Californian who has played Pebble innumerable times dating back to the U. S. Amateur in 1947; he won the Crosby in 1961. He thinks the course plays tougher when the sun is out and it's windy and dry underfoot. He points out that, when the course gets dry and hard, it is extremely difficult to get the ball on the green and keep it there. He cites the two-over-par score of 290 with which Nicklaus won the U. S. Open by three shots in 1972 as proof that the course is harder in clear and windy weather. I agree.

Starting with the seventh hole, you face four holes that are the toughest consecutive holes I have ever seen. I know if I leave the sixth green anything worse than even par, I'm likely to have a bad round.

The eighth hole can play almost any way, with distance a widely varying factor. I've seen times when you had to hit an iron off the tee to avoid driving it too far. Then, under those circumstances with a gale at your back, you have a devil of a time keeping the ball on the green with the second shot. At other times, when the wind turns around, you are going at it with a driver and a four-wood, full tilt. It changes with the weather and is a tremendous hole.

The drive is blind, with the green out of sight from the teeing ground. There is a chimney on a home in the background and, if you hit the ball toward the chimney, you will be on the fairway. Through the years, I've felt that a drive to the right of the chimney gives you a better shot at the green. It's a spectacular view when you come to the top of the hill. The next shot is across a canyon and the edge of the ocean—one big ravine. After driving to the right of center, club selection is dictated by the wind and its direction.

Bob Rosburg hits shot across chasm and water to green.

View of rugged cliffside below player approaching green.

You must hit across that chasm and water to a well-trapped green that is cut into the slope on the other side.

Bob Rosburg has been a good friend for many years. We started on the tour at about the same time. Once considered a good baseball prospect when he was at Stanford, Rosburg chose golf instead, although he kept his somewhat unorthodox "baseball grip"—that is, he does not overlap any of his fingers but has both thumbs off the shaft of the club.

Until winning the Bob Hope Classic in 1972, Rossie had gone eleven years since his Crosby win without a victory, although challenging many times. At Houston in the 1969 Open championship, he missed a four-foot putt on the final hole that would have tied Orville Moody, the winner. Bob's biggest victory was in the 1959 PGA championship in Minneapolis.

Bob has alternated between club jobs and the tour in recent years and, during one tenure at a club job, won the National Club Pro championship at Pinehurst. Bob is bright and witty and a good companion, except immediately after a poor round. His competitive spirit sometimes gets the best of him briefly in such circumstances. But he settles down quickly and is fun to be around.

On the day we played, both our drives were in good shape to the right of center of the fairway. The pin was in its most difficult position—to the right. Rosburg's four-wood shot was excellent, the ball rolling to the back of the putting surface. I hit a three-iron that drifted a little right and plugged near the lip of the bunker that guards the front of the green. I just managed to get my ball out of the sand and put it on the fringe of the green some forty feet from the hole. Rosburg putted well from the back edge for a tap-in par; then I got lucky and made my putt for a half.

Arnold Palmer plays trap shot with Bob Rosburg looking on.

To score well on this hole, our low-handicap golfer must drive it straight and long—a tough assignment. As many low men tend to hook the ball, his second shot could be next to impossible if the wind is in his face. It often is. The low man still wants to try for the green regardless of how long a second shot he has. It could mean disaster. On a hole like this one, with less than a perfect drive, the low handicapper should not try for the green. He should play his second into the fairway that swings in to the green from the left and try to wedge it close for a par. That way, the imminent double or triple bogey is eliminated.

Our middle man is in fairly good shape on this hole, if he plays around the chasm. A drive and an iron should get him within seven-iron distance of the green. He should escape with a bogey, or perhaps one-putt for a par, although it is a tough, two-level green.

Our high man is in trouble again. He has to dribble the ball around the left side away from the chasm and will need four or five shots to make the green. Still, if he two-putts, he might tie the low handicappers who have gambled and lost.

Before we parted, I asked Rosburg about his three-week suspension in the summer of 1973.

"I think I kind of overstepped my bounds, I guess. Probably, the suspension was warranted. It came about because I discussed an internal problem of the TPD [Tournament Players' Division] with the news media and it didn't come out quite the way I wanted it. But I said it and I can't say I got a bad deal.

"Being a member of the policy board on and off since 1959, I have always said what I thought. I thought the rules were being flaunted and I said so. Slow play has been enforced more since the incident, so maybe it helped indirectly."

That's the way Bob Rosburg is and that's why he is one of the men who has helped shape the tour. You never have to wonder what he's thinking.

The Champions Golf Club

HOUSTON, TEXAS

14th HOLE, 430 YARDS, PAR 4

Although the golf course is less than twenty years old, the Champions has hosted more than its share of tournaments, including the National Open championship won by Orville Moody in 1969. The course was carved out of the Houston countryside some twenty-five miles from downtown and has matured so rapidly it seems as if it has always been there.

The course was built by Jimmy Demaret and Jack Burke, a pair of natives who made headlines on the golf tour for many years. Demaret has been called by Ben Hogan "the greatest shotmaker who ever played," and Burke won both the PGA and the Masters in the same year, 1956, and once won four tournaments in a row while on the tour.

"Both Jimmy and I were getting to where we were shooting it off the scoreboard on the circuit, so it was time for us to find a new kind of business," says Burke. "We decided, since we were both born in Houston, to build a good golf course there. One that we could be proud of and that would stand the test of championship play.

"I think you are going to see a lot of this in years to come . . . professionals building golf courses . . . and I honestly think American golfers are going to get better golf courses to play on."

Burke and Demaret went about designing the Champions in a unique way. Feeling that there is too much sand on most courses, they built the Champions first without a sand bunker anywhere, reasoning that you must play a course first to know just exactly where to penalize a player and also, and more important, where not to penalize him.

"Another thing," explained Burke, "in building a golf course, if you put in the sand right away, there is a lot of erosion, so we just let the mounds more or less grass themselves over. Then we played the course and could see where the sand could be put to the best use."

The fourteenth at the Champions is a most demanding hole. Not only must the tee shot be perfectly placed, but the second shot cannot stray, either.

The championship tee is between 440 and 450 yards from the middle of the green. The left side of the fairway is densely populated by trees, and the approach to the green from that side is guarded by an overhanging tree, which forces anyone playing from the left-hand side to try to hook the ball around it to get to the putting surface. Obviously it's not the place to be.

The right-hand side is also heavily wooded but is really guarded by a huge tree that is 280 yards from the tee. The ideal target when the pin is on the left side of the green (it usually is) is about ten to twenty yards left of that tree. This puts you in the right center of the fairway, takes the tree guarding the green out of play, and opens up the hole.

The green is heart-shaped, with the bottom of the heart pointing to the left. A bunker separates the two curves on the back right, and there is a contour in the green that practically bisects it. From the right, you must putt downhill; from left of center, you have a level putt.

Then, making the hole even more difficult, a pond protects the left front and side of the green. The pond starts from the right center in front of the green and winds all the way around to the back left. You can imagine how much of a hazard this is when you consider that the slope of the green moves the ball to the left most of the time when it lands, particularly accentuating any hooked or pulled approach. And remember, most good players have hooking action.

For the low handicapper, par there is quite a challenge. Usually he has right-to-left action. That's the way most good players learn the game. Since most of the trouble on the hole is to the left, including that water at the green, our low handicapper is intimidated as soon as he steps onto the championship tee. As often as not in this state of mind, he will proceed to drive either into the right woods—failing to hook—or somewhere in the left side of the fairway.

Now he has his troubles. The overhanging limb is right in his line of

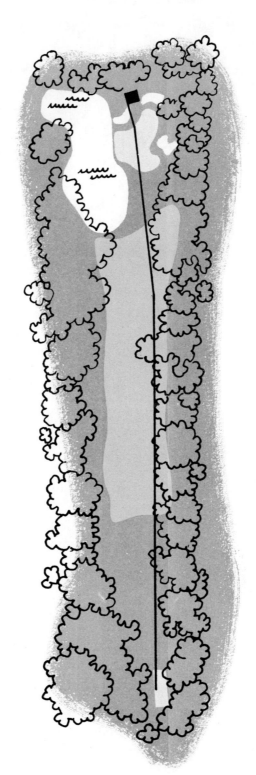

The Champions Golf Club
Houston, Texas
14th Hole, Par 4

Ben Crenshaw
tees off.

flight. He can't go over the tree with a four- or five-iron, so must hook the ball around the tree. Hooking the ball, as we said before, is no problem for the good player but, if the ball bounces left when it hits the green, more than likely it will bounce right off the green into the water.

If the hook doesn't come off, the ball will either fly over the green or to the right, where three bunkers wait to catch errant shots. Now he is faced with a trap shot that is delicate, to say the least. If he strikes the ball too hard, he puts the ball in the water; if he is light, he has his hands full getting down in two.

The medium handicapper is in good shape on this hole because he is not expected to par it. For the most part, he slices his wood shots and is fairly accurate with the short irons and the putter. The hole was made for him to score an easy five and, occasionally, a par-four.

Assuming he starts the ball from the regular tee some 40 yards in front of the championship tee, he has to traverse some 400 yards. His drive, with the big slice, travels in the neighborhood of 160 to 180 yards. It must surely land somewhere on the right side of the fairway. He may even be too far right and be blocked by the big tree on that side.

The tree, which would present an insurmountable problem for our low handicapper and a difficult one for our professional players, is made to order for old Mr. Medium. In fact, he can use it as a guideline. Making sure he aims well to the right of the tree, our medium man hits a three-wood that arches in a parabola around the tree and comes to rest some fifty to seventy-yards from the green on the right side of the fairway, away from the water and with a clear pitch shot to just any of many possible difficult pin placements.

Unfortunately, the same isn't true of the high handicapper. Even from the front tee, he will not be able to move the ball anywhere that would give him a decent second shot. Assuming he has sliced, his second shot might also slice, and he would be in the right woods. If he bloops the ball, it also could wind up in those trees.

The percentage way for the high man to play the hole is to hit two iron shots—say, a four- or five-iron. This should keep him straight and move the ball some two hundred yards up the fairway. Then he can opt for a fairway wood or another iron and aim for the right side of the fairway. His fourth shot is the toughest one for him, as he has to either carry a bunker or the water, so the closer he is to the green, the better his chances.

I remember the hole well, having played it many times in tour tournaments, in the Ryder Cup matches (1967), and in the Open championship. I had real hopes for the Open there since I won the first big tournament ever held on the course (Houston Champions International in the fall of 1966) and played well in the Ryder Cup matches.

In one round Julius Boros and I were five down at the turn. Jack Burke walked up to me and said he'd buy me a homemade watch if Boros and I could beat the Englishmen. I still have that watch, and Burke still thinks we bamboozled him on the score.

In the 1969 Open, I made four straight birdies on the first hole, all from off the green, and really thought I would get a charge going each day. But the course is so demanding that you have to be at your super best to beat it. I never could get it going, although I was in contention until I three-putted the fifteenth green in the last round. I got through the fourteenth with a par, but, to give you an idea of how a course can change, I had to hit a three-iron to the green in that round after a fairly good drive.

My playing companion for the filmed round at Champions, Ben Crenshaw, is headed for superstardom. He came out on the tour right off the campus of the University of Texas with three NCAA championships under his belt and in less than three years won three tournaments and upward of $300,000. Ben never won the U. S. Amateur championship, but that's about the only thing he didn't win before turning professional.

I have talked to Ben about his start on the tour and how I felt when I started out in 1955. I asked him how old he was that year and he said he was three years old. That made me feel like an old man, but, like Ben, it was what I always wanted to do.

Crenshaw plays for titles, not for money. The good players are the ones who win the cups and trophies—the money follows, as Crenshaw already knows. He says he has felt like he has been stealing, it has been so much fun. That's a great attitude.

The day Ben and I played the fourteenth hole, the prevailing wind that usually blows from left side to the right was not in evidence. It was a good thing, too, as that makes the hole about 25 per cent more difficult, and I doubt if we could have played it as well as we did.

We both had super drives down the right center of the fairway—Position A. I had a seven-iron to the green, considerably less club than under normal, windy circumstances. Ben hit an eight-iron.

My ball was about fifteen feet from the pin, just outside Crenshaw's. I made a bad first putt but got a par. Crenshaw dumped his putt in the hole for a birdie.

I told Ben that we paid all the professionals a fee to appear on the show, but I couldn't even buy him dinner or I would wreck his amateur standing. Actually, I put the fee in a golf scholarship fund and Crenshaw turned pro a few months later.

Scioto Country Club

COLUMBUS, OHIO

2nd HOLE, 439 YARDS, PAR 4

Scioto Country Club in Columbus, Ohio, has one of the toughest par-four holes in the world. The second hole has a slight dogleg to the right, and the fairway is at its tightest where the tee ball lands.

The right is protected by bunkers that cannot be carried by even the longest hitters, and the left is tree-lined all the way to the green. Beyond the bunkers on the right is a downslope and out of bounds.

Add to that an elevated oval green that slopes slightly toward the player, bunkered both left and right with a small opening in the center, and you have one tough cookie. Also, the fairway is hog-backed, so shots to the left go farther left after landing, and shots to the right go farther off line in that direction when they bounce.

This is where Jack Nicklaus learned to play golf. No wonder he learned to hit it long. He had to or not play. Tom Weiskopf, also a long hitter, says it is the hardest driving hole he knows. You not only have to hit it long, but you must also hit it straight.

After a drive that lands between the bunkers and the trees at the dogleg, where the fairway is not more than thirty-five yards wide, you still have a long way to go. A good five-iron should make the green, but you do not want to get above the pin and face a downhill putt on a fast green.

61

Our low handicapper has poor odds on his drive. If he draws it, he will wind up in the woods. Unless he is dead straight, the bunkers grab him. He then will have to play a recovery shot before going at the green to try to salvage par. A tough order. More likely a six.

Our middle man is all right here. His first wood shot is short of the bunkers, and his second slice follows the route of the dogleg. He then has a seven-iron to the green and two putts for a five.

Our high handicapper might get through the troubles in three shots. Then he may have as many as three more to the green, if he avoids the traps. Two putts and he is safely down in eight. Bravo.

The Country Club of Detroit

GROSSE POINTE FARMS, MICHIGAN

18th HOLE, 425 YARDS, PAR 4

I played probably the most important shot of my amateur career on the eighteenth hole at the Country Club of Detroit. In the semifinal round of the U. S. Amateur championship, I was all even with Ed Meister of Cleveland coming to this final hole.

I hit a four-iron over the green, and Meister was fifteen feet below the pin with a good birdie chance. My ball was almost blocked by a tree, with the green six feet high in front of me, sloping away. Nobody in the gallery gave me a chance.

I managed somehow to get my wedge under the ball with plenty of backspin and stopped the ball three feet above the hole. Meister missed his birdie, I holed, and I went on to beat him on the third extra hole.

The next day I beat Bob Sweeney for my first major title. It set the stage for me to turn professional a few weeks later.

The hole is a demanding one in that trees guard the green and the target area is small. Also, trees line the left side of the fairway and bunkers the right.

Our low handicapper again will have trouble placing his tee ball and fairly often will go left into the trees. If he aims too far to the right, he en-

63

counters bunker trouble. With an ordinary drive, he needs a two- or a three-iron to get home. A bogey is not out of the ordinary.

Our middle handicapper will slice the ball short of the bunkers, slice the three-wood somewhere short of the green, and wedge to the green. Probably five, possibly four.

Our high handicapper will take about four shots to reach the green, if he can avoid the fairway bunker and the traps around the green. That means he will score five or six. Not bad.

Aronomink Golf Club

PHILADELPHIA, PENNSYLVANIA

1st HOLE, 432 YARDS, PAR 4

I have often thought how important the PGA championship at Aronomink in 1962 could have been to me. It was played the week after the British Open, which I won at Troon, and I mused on the way back over the Atlantic that I could make it my biggest year ever.

Even though I had lost the U. S. Open playoff at Oakmont, I had the Masters and British Open titles of 1962. If I could win at Aronomink, I would have a new "triple" and could say that I had finished first in the "Big Four" in one year.

But my old pal, Gary Player, took the show away from me. And he made his move every day on the first hole.

In those days Gary used a four-wood off the tee on occasions, especially when he wanted to hook it. The first hole at Aronomink was the perfect place for Player to use it.

The hole has a lot of trouble on the left side, but the right side slopes toward the fairway. But if you hit it too far to the right, it's amen. On all four days, Gary started the ball far to the right, and the gallery would moan, thinking it was gone. Then it would hook back into the middle of the fairway, and Player was off and running.

After a decent tee shot, a four-iron or more is required to get home. Putting is a sometime thing, but this green was in perfect shape. I remember making two birdies there.

Our low handicapper has the hole measured to order. He crushes his tee shot, gets a light hook, and is dead center in the fairway. A midiron to the green, easy par, a chance for birdie.

Our middle handicapper is not so fortunate. His most-of-the-time slice will catch the right rough, and his second will be well short of the green. A long iron is next, and a six looms on the horizon.

Our high man, with his visual wildness, is in trouble on this tight hole. The chances are that he'll take five to reach the green. We hope he one-putts here so that he can have at least one double bogey on his card for respect.

Belle Meade Country Club

NASHVILLE, TENNESSEE

4th HOLE, 301 YARDS, PAR 4

Leave it to the home of country music to come up with a "little ole cute hole" that's as mean as a hunted rattler yet gives the appearance of a lady in gingham and crinoline.

The 301-yard over-all length of the fourth hole at Belle Meade in Nashville means nothing, since you cannot tee it up and drive for the green. The fairway is a three-quarter island, and the green is protected by a creek. Trees obscure the green from the tee and make it impossible to drive it because they are too high.

So you drive it over the creek and shoot over the trees to the green and root for getting it close.

In an exhibition I played there with Mason Rudolph, Jack Nicklaus, and Waxo Green of the Nashville *Banner*, I remember asking Mason what to do. He suggested a two-iron aimed to the right, even though the left side shortens the yardage.

I hit a two-iron and a wedge, made a four, and was happy that I hadn't seen the hole before. The creek winds all around that island fairway and comes in play everywhere.

A low handicapper would play it about the same way I did, except he would probably aim more to the right and go over the creek to the green with a nine-iron.

The middle handicapper would hit his driver and be in good position for an eight- or nine-iron second shot and a possible birdie try unless he misses one of the shots completely.

There is another tee for the high handicapper that moves him closer to the water. Depending how many shots it takes him to carry the creek both times, you can name a score. It is possible for him to carry the creek, play up safe, carry the creek the second time, and have a putt for a par, but I doubt it.

Colonial Country Club

FORT WORTH, TEXAS

5th HOLE, 459 YARDS, PAR 4

The fifth hole at Colonial Country Club in Forth Worth, Texas, ranks high among the celebrated non-TV holes in the country. Because this tough, par-four hole, hard by a meandering branch of the Trinity River, is so distant from the television cameras, only the on-the-scene spectators who hoof it know much about it.

However, nearly every great player has experienced the rigors of the hole, and many have wished they hadn't. I consider it a great hole because, sooner or later, you must play a difficult shot.

The temptation is to play it safe off the tee with a three-wood or one-iron, what with the river flowing so close to the right side and a ditch with overhanging trees on the left edge of the fairway at the landing area where the hole doglegs to the right. But this leaves you with a shot of more than 200 yards to a narrow, two-level green surrounded by bunkers.

I usually go with my driver, even though the landing area is no more than 35 yards wide. Once in a while, you will hit a bad one, but it's best to go with the club that gives you the best chance. On this hole, the driver is it. Even when I hit a good tee ball, I'm still faced with 180 to 190 yards to that well-bunkered green with its two levels. I'll take par there any time.

The low handicapper probably should lay up and keep the ball in play, unless he has command of a controlled fade with his driver. In any event, he will have a long second shot, and it will likely take a wedge shot and a one-putt green to rescue a par.

The middle handicapper may need three wood shots to get home. If he is accurate, he has a chance for a five, thereby avoiding the seven or eight that he would normally get at the fifth.

Our high handicapper may take as many as ten strokes on this hole, even if he is playing well that particular day. There is really no safe way home for him. Sticking with his irons will at least minimize the damage.

Doral Golf and Country Club

MIAMI, FLORIDA

BLUE COURSE, 18th HOLE, 437 YARDS, PAR 4

Each week on the golf telecasts, someone invariably will say: "This is one of the toughest finishing holes in golf." The eighteenth at Doral really is.

The wind is usually dead against you, and especially stiff in the afternoon, when you are trying to finish your round. There is a lake all the way from the tee to the green, and the fairway on the left slopes into the lake.

On the right side, there are enough trees to be bothersome and, faced with a long shot, they can get in the way physically and even psychologically. Yet the ball should be driven to the right side of the fairway, not only to stay away from the water but also to avoid a second shot over the water to the green and the pin, which is often tucked back left. The green is 175 feet deep. I have seen the hole played with a two-iron second in the wind but, when it's calm, with a seven- or eight-iron. The green is treacherous because if you do not get all the way to the putting surface, the ball usually goes into the water. In fact, it is possible to draw the ball off the green into the water. The slope is that steep.

A low-handicap player should aim right, even at the rough, and take his chances on a good lie and a clear shot. On his second shot, he has to take enough club to insure flying the ball to the green, aiming well to the right, al-

71

though a bunker may catch him there. That route should eliminate the double bogey.

The middle handicapper is in good shape for a bogey-five. He cannot reach the green in two strokes and cannot go in the water unless he hits his once-a-week hook shot. A nine-iron or wedge into the green and two putts will give him a five.

Our high handicapper can just dribble the ball down the right side, on in five and two putts for a seven. Maybe one putt this time.

Pinehurst Country Club

PINEHURST, NORTH CAROLINA

NO. 2 COURSE,
5th HOLE, 440 YARDS, PAR 4

Pinehurst, a famous name in golf, has long been a mecca of amateur activity. I played much of my amateur golf at Pinehurst, where I first met fellows like Frank Stranahan and Harvie Ward, my most talented opponents until I turned professional.

I have always liked Donald Ross courses, and Pinehurst No. 2 may be his monument. The first time you go around it, the subtleties may be concealed, yet the more you play the course, the more you realize the demand for placement and position, as well as length.

There are many great holes there but, to me, the fifth could be the best par-four of its kind. When you go to the fifth tee, you are back in the wooded pines that abound there. The hole opens up wide in front of you.

At least that's what it seems like. What you don't realize is that, while the fairway opens up, there are quite a few obstacles. First of all, the fairway slopes severely to the left into rough and trees. From the left rough, trees almost completely block you from going for the green.

If you go too far to the right, you face an extremely long second shot, and you must carry a bunker that guards the green. Add to this a hill to the left of the green and you have a treacherous hole.

I used to try to place my ball on the right center of the fairway so I

73

would not have a downhill lie to an uphill green. Then a three- or four-iron would get the job done.

Our low handicapper has to have a superior drive, and even so will most likely hit it left if it's not pluperfect. Then the difficult second shot either goes into the sand or is well off the green to the left. He would be better off not trying to crush the tee shot, playing the right side. A good chip and putt might save par.

Our middle handicapper plays for a five and an occasional four, since his slice keeps him in the right or safe side. He can get close with two wood shots and, depending on his wedge and putter, he scores five.

Our high handicapper, if he can keep the ball straight, gets home in four or five strokes. With two putts, his best score would be no better than a six.

Harbour Town Golf Links

HILTON HEAD, SOUTH CAROLINA

18th HOLE, 458 YARDS, PAR 4

The final hole at Hilton Head's Harbour Town links might just be the most demanding finishing hole in golf, since par is four and the distance is 458 yards. That is only part of it, however. In order to negotiate the hole in two shots, the water of Calibogue Sound must be traversed twice.

The Sound runs along the hole on the left, and some of the prettiest pine and palmetto trees I've ever seen form a forest on the right.

You can carry the water off the tee to a peninsula fairway or you can flirt with the woods on the right. The choice to go to the right precludes reaching the green in regulation. In either event, it will take two wood shots because a huge bunker lies directly in front of the green. A most difficult par.

Our low handicapper is in trouble here because of the demand on accuracy. He more than likely will try the peninsula landing zone. The slightest hooking action and he will be in the Sound. Even if he does hit a superior tee shot, his next task is the same—no hooking.

Our low handicapper might be wiser to hit a three-wood safely to the right of the tee, an iron to the right of the green, and depend on his chipping and putting for his par. Otherwise, double bogey or worse is his fate.

Our middle man should manage a five. Avoiding the water, he puts his tee ball somewhere near the forest. His sliced second stays on the right side of the fairway, and his third shot is about a seven-iron to the green. If he doesn't get too bold about pin placements and just lands the ball on the green, he has the five with two putts.

Our high handicapper may play this hole until dark unless he "bunts" the ball from tee to green. Maybe he should quit at seventeen.

The Homestead

CASCADES COURSE, UPPER COURSE, 10th HOLE, 377 YARDS, PAR 4

The tenth hole of the Cascades Course at the Homestead in Hot Springs has a severe dogleg to the right. Along the right side of the fairway from the tee to the landing area is a ravine about a hundred feet deep, full of trees, underbrush, and lost golf balls.

The drive is the important shot here. There is little room on the left side to play safe and, when you do, you add about fifty yards to your second shot.

A long drive can carry through the fairway into the rough, increasing the difficulty of the next shot. The best shot is a three-wood to the middle of the fairway, which puts you on the hill overlooking the green to the right. If you hit through the hill, either the rough or a downhill lie will penalize you.

A six- or seven-iron second will be sufficient to reach the green from your location high above the green.

The green is a well-trapped affair, and like all Hot Springs putting surfaces, full of tricky breaks that are almost indiscernible. It is almost mandatory to get close to make a birdie.

Our low handicapper, if he doesn't try to bust a drive, can play a spoon carefully to the center or left of the fairway. From there a five- or six-iron shot will be the key to his birdie possibilities.

77

Our middle handicapper has little chance because of his slicing action. Try as he might to keep the ball left, the sliced tee shot will invariably either go over the cliff or hang up on the edge near the trees, since the fairway does slope left. He then must hit another shot into the blind, hoping for a decent lie for his chip to the green. Usually a six for our middle man and his left-to-right play.

Our high handicapper plays down the left side on his first two shots, hits his next down the hill, and then tries to reach the green through rough and traps. I figure it will be five or six before he is on, and then two putts.

Pittsburgh Field Club

FOX CHAPEL, PENNSYLVANIA

12th HOLE, 459 YARDS, PAR 4

The Pittsburgh Field Club has a unique distinction. It was a featured part of an Open championship, yet has never hosted the championship proper.

In 1954, it was decided to have two qualifying rounds at the scene of the championship, so a round each was played at Oakmont and the Field Club. Surprisingly, the qualifying scores were higher at the Field Club, and a lot of the woe was caused by the twelfth hole.

The teeing area is hard by Fox Chapel Road but surrounded by trees so that the cars whizzing by do not disturb the long hitters. The right side of the fairway is the short way home but is perilously close to some of the worst rough to be found anywhere.

From the right side of the fairway, a long iron will sometimes suffice, although, on windy days, the hole demands all you can hit.

In an exhibition there in the long ago, Sam Snead once had to hit two drivers to reach the green. As he walked up after the second shot, he cracked: "I bet all the members get home here in two."

The left side of the fairway has rough, bunkers, and a three-foot ledge along with plenty of trees to hamper the errant left-side shot.

Our low handicapper more than likely will hit the fairway somewhere left of center and then will try a spoon to a well-trapped green, both left and right. He will either have a bunker shot or a difficult chip to try to make par.

Our middle handicapper will slice his way down the right side, more than likely catching the right bunker with his third shot. From there it is a matter of two or three shots for a six.

Our high handicapper will not find this hole overly challenging. Four of his semiwhiffies will get him in the vicinity of the green. From there he can chip and two-putt for a seven.

PGA National Golf Club

PALM BEACH GARDENS, FLORIDA

EAST COURSE, 18th HOLE, 421 YARDS, PAR 4

Now that the National PGA has divorced itself from its swanky head-quarters of a decade at Palm Beach Gardens, the golf courses there probably have seen their last national action. But the excellent East Course enjoyed its share of tournament excitement while the honeymoon with owner John D. MacArthur was still on.

Jack Nicklaus won his second PGA championship there in 1971 and teamed with me to take the second National Team championship (then called Four-ball championship) in 1966. It is a tough golf course, another excellent Dick Wilson layout with a finishing hole as demanding to par as just about any I have encountered. In fact, with a birdie Bill Casper almost sneaked up on Nicklaus in that PGA championship, something like what Casper did to me in the 1966 Open at Olympic Club.

The eighteenth, a par-four measuring 421 yards, has trouble everywhere. Since the wind is usually against the player, you have to risk the narrow driving position between bunkers to the right and a finger of a lake to the left. Lay up short of the water and you aren't likely to reach the green safely in regulation. It's a long distance over more water to an elevated green with three traps in front, one on each side and more of the water to the left and behind.

81

Casper's birdie put Nicklaus in the position of needing two pars to win the PGA outright. Jack got his birdie at the par-five seventeenth and remarked later, "I didn't want to go to that last hole needing a par to win. It's just too tough a hole."

Just as he had in each of the three earlier rounds, Nicklaus missed the green with his approach. (He had one-putted twice for pars and taken a bogey there.) However, he was just on the fringe, chipped close, and holed for his two-stroke victory.

Jack and I had a more comfortable feeling about the eighteenth on the final day of the National Team championship we won at the PGA National. We had outdistanced our closest pursuers—Doug Sanders and Al Besselink—by the time we reached the eighteenth green. When I holed a fifteen-footer for a birdie there, it gave us a 29 on that nine, a 64 for the day, and a 256 for the tournament, and victory by three strokes.

Merion Golf Club, Ardmore, Pennsylvania—East Course, 13th hole.
View of traps at green with natural growth typical of Merion.

Bay Hill Club, Orlando, Florida—17th hole. Low-level panorama shot.

*Augusta National Golf Club, Augusta, Georgia—12th hole.
Unusual low-level view across Rae's Creek toward green from
spot at water's edge to golfer's left in front of tee.*

Inverness Club

TOLEDO, OHIO

5th HOLE, 436 YARDS, PAR 4

To cite it as a Donald Ross creation endorses the playing characteristics of the golf course of the Inverness Club about as strongly as possible. The fine club in Toledo, Ohio, simply reeks with character, and the naturalness of the course almost defies description.

The fifth hole at Inverness, a 436-yard par-four, sits on a rise at the outer fringe of the property. The green is perched on high ground beyond a depression that runs through the course.

A stream flows along the right side of the driving area, yet that is the preferred side of the fairway into which the tee shot should be placed. A slope protrudes into the fairway on the left side, forcing a long second shot off an uphill lie if the creek side is avoided.

Inverness is steeped in tradition and has been the scene of numerous championships. It also was the home base for many years of Frank Stranahan, who was one of the best amateurs of the post-World War II era, even though he never won our Amateur championship.

When the U. S. Open was played at Inverness in 1920, S. P. Jermain, the club president, invited the professionals to use the clubhouse for the first time. As a token of their appreciation, the pros gave Inverness a huge grandfather's clock. It sits in the club today, bearing its inscription: "God measures men by what they are, not what they in wealth possess."

Bob Jones played in his first Open championship at the age of eighteen at Inverness, tying for eighth place: Inverness also was the scene of the first Open for Jack Nicklaus, then a chunky seventeen-year-old. That was the 1957 championship, the last time the Open was played at the Toledo club. Dick Mayer was the winner, defeating Cary Middlecoff in a playoff after a tournament that started amid a destructive storm the first day. Inverness hosted the U. S. Amateur in 1973, when Craig Stadler took the title.

The earlier Open champions at Inverness were Ted Ray in 1920 and Billy Burke in 1931. Ray, forty-three when he won, was the last British golfer to win our Open until Tony Jacklin did it a half century later. The 1931 tournament was played during a heat wave, and wouldn't you know that it would be the longest Open in history. Burke and George Von Elm were tied after seventy-two holes and went through two thirty-six-hole playoffs before Billy won by a single shot, 149–148 to 149–149.

At 6,765 yards, Inverness is not a monster course. But with greens that make the surface of an ice-skating rink seem sluggish and with 110 bunkers, it puts heavy demands on every phase of the player's game.

Par Threes

The par-three is the darling of the galleries, club players, women, and children because, for the most part, it can be seen from start to finish and can be reached in one stroke. It's the one hole that just about every golfer can reach in regulation.

The possibility of a hole-in-one is constantly in everyone's mind, from duffer to professional, since it is the lucky bounce, more often than not, that decides if the ball goes in the hole.

I have tried to select par-threes that range from nine-irons to wood shots in length, showing the variety that can be attained by an architect in the design stage.

Unfortunately, during the play of these holes, none of us recorded a hole-in-one. I could have really written about that one.

So let's turn to the glamor hole of golf, the par-three.

Merion Golf Club

ARDMORE, PENNSYLVANIA

EAST COURSE, 13th HOLE, 129 YARDS, PAR 3

Merion, the famous course in Philadelphia's Main Line, has hosted the U. S. Open championship three times, but holds a prestigious place in golf history more because of what happened several years before the first Open was staged there.

At the age of fourteen, Bobby Jones made his national competitive debut at Merion in the U. S. Amateur championship. Fourteen years later, Jones arrived at Merion for another National Amateur, that time with three legs up on the never-before-achieved Grand Slam. Already that year he had won the British Open and Amateur and the U. S. Open at Interlachen.

Jones swept through the field at Merion to complete the Slam, a feat that I feel certain will never be equaled. I say this because, whenever an amateur comes along today who is good enough to have the chance to do it, he is too good to remain an amateur. The pro tour is just too attractive from a financial standpoint for him to stay in the amateur ranks.

Jack Nicklaus, I think, would have had the chance to achieve the Grand Slam had he chosen to remain an amateur, but nobody since then. There are just too many fine professionals to beat in the two Opens these days, many more than Jones had to beat in 1930.

I had my sights set on a professional Grand Slam earlier in my career. I

Merion Golf Club Ardmore, Pennsylvania
East Course, 13th Hole, Par 3

Aerial view of hole from above tee.

know I had a chance to do it—win the two Opens, the Masters, and the PGA in the same year. In fact, in 1960, I won the first two and had a good shot at the third, the British Open. But I had too much trouble with the famous "road hole"—the seventeenth—at St. Andrews and finished a stroke behind winner Kel Nagle.

Merion is unique in many ways. The first tee is virtually a patio off the porch of the clubhouse. It's so close that a golfer with a particularly long, flat backswing is liable to knock a pot of tea off a luncheon table. The final three holes play through an old stone quarry. Many of the bunkers have wild growths of Scotch broom amid smooth expanses of sand. And there are no flagsticks on the greens. Well, not flagsticks as we know them. The pins are topped with pear-shaped, red wicker baskets, another Merion bow to the golfing traditions of the game's Scottish forebears.

Golf was not even in the picture when the Merion Cricket Club was founded in 1865, nobody then anticipating what a prominent place in the history of golf Merion would occupy today. It was strictly cricket, then cricket and tennis in those early years. The club didn't even have a golf course until 1896, and the present East Course didn't come into being on a 127-acre, L-shaped tract of farmland until 1910. Yet it remained known as Merion

Close-up view of green emphasizing sand traps.

Cricket Club until 1956, when the separate Merion Golf Club was structured.

What this fine course tells us today is that touch and control are as important as power in golf, although the combination is unbeatable.

The thirteenth at Merion proves one point. A par-three hole doesn't have to be 230 yards over water to be difficult. The shot is a nine-iron onto a concave green, superbly trapped. It is a demanding task to get the ball close to the hole because the green is so narrow.

If you hit the ball a little too hard, you are in the big back trap. Hit it a little too easy and you are in the sand in front. This is bad for the morale on a hole like this. If you don't have a birdie putt there, what are you doing on the tour? Yet the smaller target makes the hole tougher than the yardage would make it seem. You must get that in your mind.

Only a true stroke will keep the ball on this green, and a pin position up front necessitates a gamble if you intend to get close to the hole. The slightest bit short and you are bunkered with an almost impossible sand shot to get close to the pin.

I hit the ball within twenty feet of the cup when I played the hole with

Raymond Floyd. Raymond hit his nine-iron too hard, and the ball buried in the bunker. He had to play the ball from the poached-egg lie and try to stop it on a green sloping away from him. He couldn't. The ball rolled well past the cup and he made four. I knocked in my putt for a birdie.

Raymond won the PGA championship at Dayton, Ohio, in 1969 in a tournament that was disabled by strikes, sitdowns, and people running out on the fairway to protest whatever they were protesting. But Raymond kept his cool and went on to win.

We finally have arrived at a hole that everybody can reach in one—pro, low handicapper, middle handicapper, and even our high man. The fact that everyone can reach it doesn't mean that it is going to be abused.

However, that is the kind of a course Merion is. Difficult for the pros but fair. It gives the amateurs, regardless of handicap, a chance because it is less than 6,600 yards at full length. Yet when Olin Dutra, the man with the arms-akimbo putting style that gave him the appearance of an octopus that had lost most of its tentacles, won Merion's first U. S. Open in 1934, he shot a 293.

The score was 287 in 1950 when Ben Hogan came back from his near-fatal highway accident to win his second Open. Limping on legs that were tied together by surgeon's twine, Hogan battled his way to a seventy-two-hole tie with the late Lloyd Mangrum and George Fazio, now a noted golf course ar-

Ray Floyd
hitting tee shot.

Arnold Palmer holes birdie putt.

chitect. Hogan, of course, won the playoff, but it is remembered as much for the devastating mental error that ruined Mangrum's hopes for a second Open title.

Lloyd, a dapper, hard-bitten guy who would be the last man you would expect to make such a mistake, was only a stroke behind Hogan when they reached the sixteenth green. As Mangrum was about to putt, a bug settled on his ball. Instinctively, he picked up the ball, blew the bug off, and replaced it. When he walked off the green, USGA officials notified him that his action had cost him a two-stroke penalty. That ended the challenges to Hogan that day.

Bay Hill Club

ORLANDO, FLORIDA

17th HOLE, 223 YARDS, PAR 3

Through the years I was never able to persuade my father to take a share of the spotlight he so richly deserved . . . and now he is gone. Milfred J. (Deacon) Palmer was responsible for getting me started in the right way in sports and life in my formative years.

I remember when I was a little boy, four or five years old, how I would ride on the tractor with him as he mowed the fairways of Latrobe Country Club. He was the course superintendent at Latrobe for fifty years. We lived right on the course.

When the Depression came, the Club needed a course superintendent more than a golf professional, so the officers made him both. He was the pro for more than forty years. Pap and his men even built the back nine at Latrobe and, in my opinion, it's a better nine than the front.

When I was filming the television show that led to the writing of this book, I was stuck for a guest at Bay Hill in Orlando, Florida, where I wanted to play the seventeenth hole, a par-three that doesn't have to take a back seat to any in the world.

Bay Hill was designed by the late Dick Wilson, whom I consider the finest of all golf architects. His subtle nuances around the greens catch the

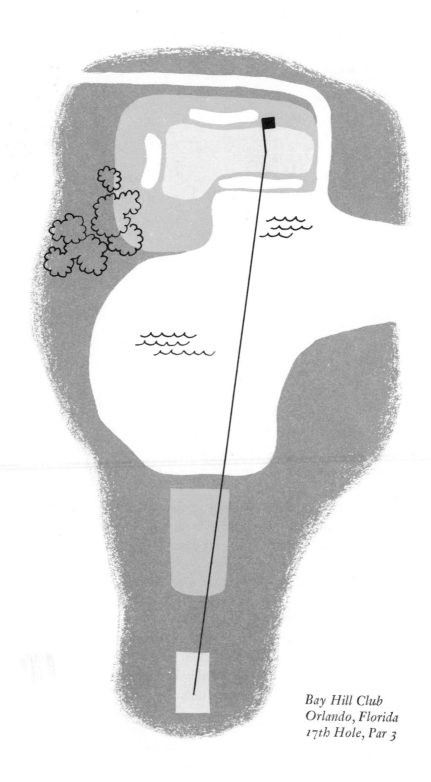

Bay Hill Club
Orlando, Florida
17th Hole, Par 3

most wary player, and he had the ability to lay out a course that utilized every bit of natural terrain.

The seventeenth is a full carry over the water, with a long, shallow trap guarding the front right two thirds of the green. Bunkers are also well placed to the left and back of the green. The green is wide and fairly shallow, with the toughest pin placements on the right side behind the water and trap. The tees are elevated.

This hole has fond memories for me. A whole gang of us were playing a rainy-day eightsome and we had all kind of little matches going among us. We came to this hole and I asked my caddy, Tom, what club to hit.

"A three-iron," Tom replied.

I hit a three-iron and hit it pretty good. It went in the water. I asked Tom what he was doing to me and took a two-iron out of the bag.

"That's too much club," Tom said. I hit the two-iron, which bounced short of the pin and went in the hole. I looked over at Tom with a smile. "No, suh, Mr. Palmer, you hit that fat," Tom said, not giving up. "I still say it's a three-iron."

All I know is I made three the hard way.

There are also one or two alligators in the lakes at Bay Hill that are often

Arnold Palmer tees off.

seen sunning themselves. And a female skin diver retrieves the many golf balls hit in the water from time to time.

One day, former Vice President Agnew, who has visited Bay Hill, hit a golf ball in the water. When he walked up to the edge of the hazard, she popped out of the water and handed him his ball. He was astounded.

On the day Pap and I went to play the seventeenth, I think that Deacon was a little nervous. I tried to relax him but really didn't have to. He smashed a good three-wood about forty feet from the pin. I've never seen a happier expression in my life. I hit a two-iron and was on the green, too, only about eight feet from the cup.

When Pap knocked the putt in for a birdie deuce, you'd think he had been a television star all of his life. He calmly walked over, picked the ball out of the hole, and looked at me. "You're away," he said. Remarking to myself that "I'd better make mine or I'll never hear the end of it," I worked pretty hard on my putt and got it in the cup for my birdie. Still, I was mighty proud of Pap for rising to the occasion as he did.

While Latrobe Country Club was Deacon's whole life, he came to admire Bay Hill as much as I have since I first played an exhibition match there back in the early 1960s when it was first opened. I had always liked that part of

Deacon "Deke" Palmer.

View from back tee to green.

Florida, which has the state's most rolling terrain, many of its lakes, and yet is far enough south to have comfortable golfing weather year 'round.

I was so attracted to Bay Hill that, in the mid-1960s, I and a small group of associates began negotiations that led to our purchase of the Club in 1969. It has become my winter home in Florida. My father and mother, Doris, who also had a great influence on my early life, enjoyed spending parts of the winter at Bay Hill. What an irony that Pap was at Bay Hill playing golf when he died in February of 1976 shortly after completing a day on the course.

Let me give you another example of how fortunate I was to have such parents when I was a boy. Once I was playing in some kind of a junior tournament in western Pennsylvania and hadn't yet learned to curb my youthful temper. I was playing badly and throwing an occasional club. When it was over and we were in the car heading home, I realized that the atmosphere was decidedly cool. Before long, Pap turned to me and, in no uncertain

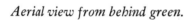

View of green as golfer sees it from front of regular tee.

Aerial view from behind green.

terms, told me: "If you ever throw a club again, I'll take them away from you. This game is for gentlemen, and gentlemen learn to control themselves." It was a very important lesson that has been so valuable to me all my life, and I say the same to any youngster, or adult, for that matter, on whom this shoe fits.

Despite its length from the back tee, the seventeenth is not overly difficult for the low handicapper, unless the wind is in his face (it often is). It's more a matter of selecting the right club because of the rather shallow depth of the green. Otherwise, he has quite a bit of room to the right or left. Our low man should be on with a long iron or, against the wind, a three- or four-wood. But don't put the middle or high handicapper on that championship tee unless you want him to admire the rather spectacular view across the water from that chute.

From the front tee, which reduces the length to about 160 to 170 yards, he can reach the green with a decent long iron or wood, even if he has that usual slice. So long as he manuevers the shot to avoid the bunkers, he can make the almost flat green and usually muster a par. Even when the pin is to the right behind the water and the long front trap, he is wise to play to the left side, since a sizable apron lies on that side beside the water short of the green. He should be able at least to make a bogey from there.

Our high handicapper might as well take a bucket of balls to that tee and keep swinging with his driver until he gets across. There is really no place for him to lay up—water to the right and several tall pines to the left short of the green that block that route. Maybe the high man ought to take the example of the 'gators and the skin diver and swim the ball across. Seriously, a bit of such frustration on that hole should convince our high handicapper that if he is going to play the game, he had better improve. He should head for the pro shop and some lessons.

Augusta National Golf Club

AUGUSTA, GEORGIA

12th HOLE, 155 YARDS, PAR 3

Cliff Roberts, who joined with Bobby Jones years ago to found the now famous Augusta National Golf Club, was elated when I told him I had picked two holes at his course among my "best."

The first one is the twelfth, probably the greatest par-three in the world. This hole—with its swirling winds hovering around a green that exposes a wide, shallow surface to the tee and is guarded by water, bunkers, and a hillside—has been the scene of many a disaster as well as many a victory in the classic Masters championship.

I asked Mr. Roberts to tell us something about the fabled hole.

"First of all, I agree with you about the twelfth hole, not only because it is here but because it is my favorite of all the holes we have here," said Cliff.

"To give you a little background, I might tell you that the reason these two holes are great, in my opinion, is because they are both nature-made holes. I recall very distinctly, because money was a little short when we built this golf course in the depth of the Depression [1930–31], that the hole cost very little money to build. It was already there.

"Bob Jones and the architect, Alistar McKenzie, just had to find the hole. It had been there forever. The only money spent was to smooth off the ledge and build the tee and plant some grass for the green.

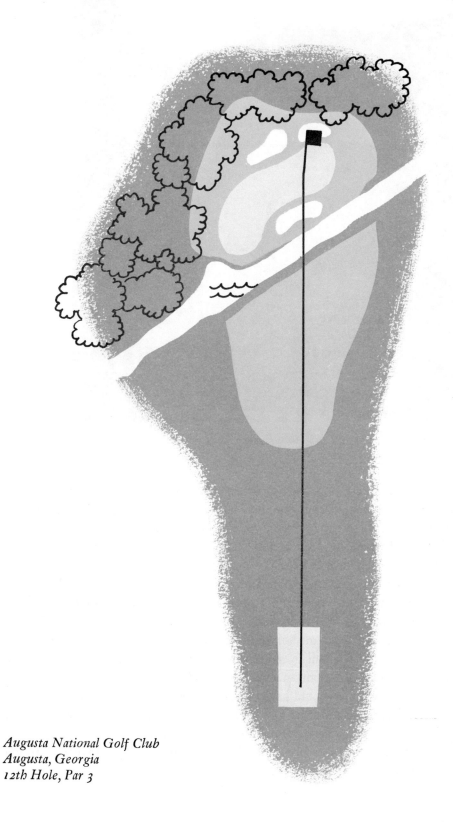

Augusta National Golf Club
Augusta, Georgia
12th Hole, Par 3

Tommy Aaron sizes up chip shot from behind green.

"Another interesting point is that the engineer who built this green discovered that No. 12 was at one time an old Indian burial ground, and maybe that the spirit of some old Indian chief is the reason that the boys are prone to be fooled when they play the hole and, instead of landing in the cemetery, the ball is spirited into the creek."

I don't know anything about Indian chiefs or spirits, but I do know that the twelfth has taken its toll more times than the golfers would care to remember. Besides an old Indian chief, a lot of players' hopes are buried there.

I have good and bad memories of No. 12.

In 1958, I hit the ball over the green and it embedded in the side of the hill, which was soft from an overnight rain. I asked for a ruling, and the official told me that I would have to play the ball where it lay. I disagreed, so I played that ball his way and made five, and another ball by placing it and made three. At the fourteenth tee, Bob Jones told me that I had made a three on the hole, that my interpretation of the rules was correct. I went on to win my first Masters.

Coming to the twelfth green in 1959, I had a five-shot lead, life was beautiful, and I was going to be the first man ever to successfully defend the Masters title. I came off the ball a little, landed in the creek, eventually took six, and all hell broke loose. I could hear the birdie roars all over the course and, despite the fact that I birdied the next hole, I finished third as Art Wall birdied six of the last seven to win, and Doc Middlecoff moved into second place.

Let me try to describe the hole as I see it from the tee. The green, as I said before, is wide and narrow as you look at it from the tee. It is shaped like a bowling pin, with the small end to the right and the big end to the left as if it were lying on its side. In competition, the pin is more often to the right-hand side, which makes club selection very difficult.

Club selection depends on pin placement, wind, type of day (on some days the air is heavier than others), and how you are playing. If things aren't

View of green from behind back trap.

going well, or you have just come off the eleventh hole with a bogey, you are apt to be less alert than if you are playing well and have just birdied No. 11.

I have played the twelfth with a seven-iron and have also used a three-iron. In one Masters years ago, Bob Rosburg selected a five-iron for his club. The wind was blowing quite hard toward the tee. As he made contact with the ball, the wind stopped and the ball carried right over the green and off the property onto the adjacent Augusta Country Club. It had to carry forty yards over the green and be at least fifty feet in the air.

"Longest five-iron I ever hit," was Rosburg's comment after he had hurled a few invectives at the gods who control the atmosphere and winds.

The difficulty is trying to stop the ball on the putting surface, which is only about twenty yards wide when the pin is on the right-hand side. You need enough club not only to get over the water hazard but also to carry a bunker that protects the green in front and yet not carry to the bunker that is in back. When you step into that back trap to hit a shot, all you can see is Rae's Creek, and even the boldest player strikes his sand shot somewhat timidly.

Let us get to the low-handicap golfer and his chances for a par at this most difficult hole. If the pin is on the left-hand side, a five-iron should be

Arnold Palmer, Tommy Aaron, and caddies on green.

View of green as Tommy Aaron studies shot.

ample. The green is much wider there and he wants to make sure he gets over the water.

If the pin is on the right-hand side, however, our low-handicap man is in trouble. There is a slope to the right of the green, so, if he takes enough club to get over the pond but leaks the shot just a bit, he finds the water over there. If he muscles the shot to make sure he carries, the ball most likely will land somewhere up the hill or in the back bunker. It takes an almost-perfect shot for the low handicapper—and with a four- or five-iron to hit the putting surface and stay on. Possible but highly improbable. He will most likely have a bunker shot—if he escapes the creek. A par here is a fine score for the low man.

Unless conditions are calm, the medium handicapper has a wood shot to the fat part of the green. If he has the usual slice, the more difficult pin placements are in his line of fire. Oddly enough, he is more apt to hit the putting surface than the low man, providing, of course, he aims to the extreme left of the green and hits the right club reasonably well.

The only problem with our medium man is distance. He must hit the four- or three-wood well to get over the water, since the slice reduces distance, and the slopes and bunker are in range of a poorly hit ball. Of course, the extreme slice will splash.

The high handicapper has little chance to get over the water with his tee shot unless there is no wind. Otherwise, his best move is to hit an iron short of the water and then worry about getting his second over. The wise choice then is to play to the fat part of the green with a wedge or nine-iron and trust his putting stroke to produce a bogey, a good score for anyone on this hole.

In the 1973 Masters, when Tommy Aaron broke through to win his first major championship and, being a Georgia boy, fulfill a lifelong dream, he made the putting surface in all four rounds. He made a birdie with a good putt the first day and par the other three rounds. Anytime you play this hole in one under par for four rounds, you are a contender because it sets you up to score on the next three holes, two of which are par-fives that can be reached in two strokes. Coming off the twelfth with a bogey, you tend to play catch-up, and that's a tough game.

The Masters, of course, is part of my life. I looked forward as a kid just to be invited to play there. Then going there and playing, seeing all the things that happen, not only to me but also to everyone, has been tremendous.

Of course, winning the tournament four times was the icing on the cake. The galleries at Augusta have been super to me. There's not another tournament in the world that gives me the same thrill. I enjoy it here as if it were home.

I played the hole for the series with Tommy Aaron. It was a typical day at Augusta National, with the wind gusting and the sun shining. Aaron hit a six-iron to the base of the hillside in back, leaving himself with a most difficult chip shot. I hit a six-iron about ten feet from the cup on the right-hand side of the green and was staring a birdie in the face.

Well, Aaron played a super chip shot and almost holed it for a two. He made the little putt and settled happily for a par. I left my putt short and missed that one for a bogey.

That proved a point I made in this chapter. Aaron had gained a stroke with his fine chip shot, and I had lost at least one and maybe two strokes with my poor first putt. Who do you think was in the better frame of mind as we went to the thirteenth tee, where the drive determines the play of the hole? It wasn't me.

Medinah Country Club

MEDINAH, ILLINOIS

NO. 3 COURSE,
2nd HOLE, 184 YARDS, PAR 3

Some of the greatest holes in the world fail to get their proper due simply because of their front-nine location on courses. When a player makes a bogey or a birdie early in a round, it isn't as dramatic as on one of the finishing holes.

Such a hole is the second on the championship No. 3 course at Medinah Country Club, a magnificent, golf-oriented plant in the western suburbs of Chicago. Almost adjacent to the second hole is another tough par-three, the celebrated seventeenth, celebrated because it has been the scene of some spectacular blow-ups through the years.

Sam Snead was on his way to tie Cary Middlecoff for the lead in the 1949 Open when Snead came to the seventeenth. He put his tee shot on the fringe of the green, only about fifteen feet from the pin. Instead of putting, Snead chipped—poorly—and took three from the edge. He lost to Middlecoff by a stroke.

Yet I'm sure that the second hole took its toll during that Open and other important events at Medinah, although few will remember who met disaster, unless it happened to them. Once, Jack Fleck four-putted the green during the Illinois Open and walked off the course shaking his head.

A whole round can be ruined by botching up the second hole of the day. When you get off to a bad start, it is tough to play catch-up.

Water lies to the left of the second green as well as all the way from the teeing ground to the putting surface. The pin placement that is enjoyed by the devil himself is at the left front of the green. If a player wants to birdie in that case, he must try to get the ball left of the center of the green, thereby flirting with the water. And if he hits it a little light, the ball can spin back off the green and into the water in front.

Actually, a player should never go for the pin there. Hit for the center of the green and root for a par or maybe a long putt to drop. Too often water holes mean double bogeys.

There is a trap on the left side that keeps many a ball from a dip in the pond. There is also a bunker on the right side of the green so that the target, where there is no trouble, is minimal.

Aerial view of 2nd hole from above tee.

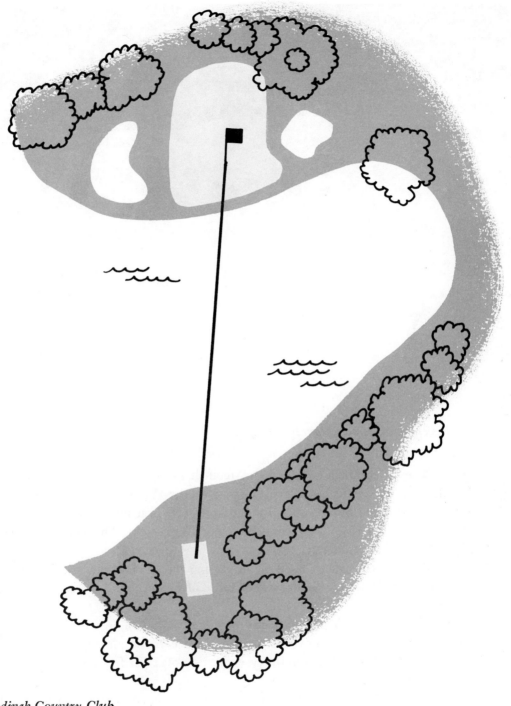

Medinah Country Club
Medinah, Illinois
No. 3 Course, 2nd Hole, Par 3

Reverse view of hole from behind green.

The U. S. Open returned to Medinah in 1975 for the first time since Middlecoff's win in 1949. Jacky Cupit won the Western Open at Medinah in 1962 and so did Billy Casper, the week after he beat me in the Open playoff at Olympic in 1966. The scores were not all that low. This golf course with all the trees is a good one.

Chi Chi Rodriguez joined me in playing the second hole, and I asked Chi Chi about his career. He has a keen sense of humor, and here is what he had to say:

"Well, I haven't played to my potential," Chi Chi answered. "I have set my goals a little too low, but one of them is to be playing until I'm Sam Snead's age. Right now I'm thirty-eight, two over par for nine holes, and I'm twenty-four years behind Sam.

"I've won seven tournaments and you've won sixty-one, you got me by fifty-four but I'm gaining on you. Don't forget I only weigh 124 pounds, so you should give me a couple of tournaments a side.

"I hit the ball very far, Arnold, because when I was a child, I learned to play golf the right way. You know, most guys don't know how to learn to play the game. I believe the way you and I and Hogan, Snead, and Nelson, the way we started as caddies, is the best way to start golf. You learn how to imitate swings, and that helps you become proficient.

"I use my legs to get clubhead speed. I have tremendous clubhead speed, and my driver is very heavy and 44½ inches long. My legs are the center of my power, and when I go home to Puerto Rico, I run about two miles in the deep sand every morning, which is great leg conditioning.

"You have to be long to play on the tour. Why, I won't even room on the tour with a short hitter. I always play practice rounds with long hitters. I think the people you associate with have a lot to do with how you hit a golf ball. That's why I like to loaf with you, Arnold."

Arnold Palmer and
Chi Chi Rodriguez.

Chi Chi is refreshing to be around but he says so many nice things about me, it's embarrassing. However, it is the dedicated people like Chi Chi who make golf such a great game.

The day we played Medinah, there was no wind. Chi Chi, who likes to hit the ball hard when the flag is on the left, hit a six-iron. He aimed to the middle of the green, figuring that, if he did pull it with the hard swing, it would wind up nearer the flagstick.

Chi Chi explained his preference for the full shot as against trying to hit a soft one, say, with a five-iron. "When you swing hard, you hit down into and through the ball. When you hit the ball easy, it often goes to the right more."

This day, Chi Chi hit a perfect six-iron to within six feet of the pin. I also used a six-iron, but it was short by about fifteen feet. I missed the putt for a par and Chi Chi rammed his home, did his little dance using the putter as a sword, and told me I was one down.

Our low handicapper is in good shape here unless he pulls or hooks the ball—a distinct possibility. He should make sure he has enough stick so he doesn't have to swing too hard. He should aim for the right center of the green to leave a margin for error. A par should be his with a well-hit five-iron.

Our middle handicapper has to figure out how much his five-wood is going to slice, so he will avoid the right bunker. With this in mind, a good swing will get him somewhere on the right side of the green. Since the green slopes dangerously toward the water, putting from the right side is a problem. He must be careful, although three-putting is probably his lot on this hole.

Our high handicapper is a pretty sure bet to lose a ball or two on this hole, since he has a lot of water to carry from the tee to the front edge of the green. However, when he hits the first one in, his drop at the edge leaves him only a hundred-yard shot to get across the water. Of course, he then has to tackle that slick, sloping green. We'll give him one ball in the water and a six on the hole.

Before leaving Medinah and Chicago, I asked Chi Chi about the work he is carrying on for the late Roberto Clemente, who played all his major-league baseball for the Pittsburgh Pirates and whom I greatly admired.

"Well, Arnold, things cannot be done without money, so that's my main objective, raising money. I know you have volunteered to play an exhibition, and we are going to take you up on it.

Aerial view of hole.

113

"Roberto died like he lived. He was a team man, and he lived as a team man and died as one. Funny, the greatest golfer in the world and the greatest baseball player with Pittsburgh ties, you and Roberto.

"If I can be half the man Roberto Clemente was, that makes me a helluva man."

Well said, Chi Chi.

Baltusrol Golf Club

SPRINGFIELD, NEW JERSEY

LOWER COURSE,
4th HOLE, 194 YARDS, PAR 3

Baltusrol is another of America's historic golf clubs and has been the scene of frequent national championships. As far back as 1903, it hosted the Open championship and Willie Anderson, a four-time Open champion along with Bobby Jones and Ben Hogan, won.

Baltusrol was host to the U. S. Open in 1915 (the winner was Jerry Travers), 1936 (Tony Manero), 1954 (Ed Furgol) and 1967 (Jack Nicklaus). There have been three U. S. Amateur championships there, too, and innumerable area championships. Jones lost his only amateur championship in a five-year span at Baltusrol in 1926 to George Von Elm, two and one.

The club was founded in 1895, seven years after the first formal golf was played in this country. Historically, the club was built on land by a man named Baltus Roll, who was murdered by two thieves supposedly searching for a large amount of money they had heard was hidden in the house atop the nearby "mountain."

This happened in 1831 and accounts for the name of the course. The original course was torn up in 1920, and two courses—the upper and the lower—were built on the land under the direction of A. G. Tillinghast, a famous golf architect at that time.

Johnny Farrell, the 1928 U. S. Open champion who defeated the great

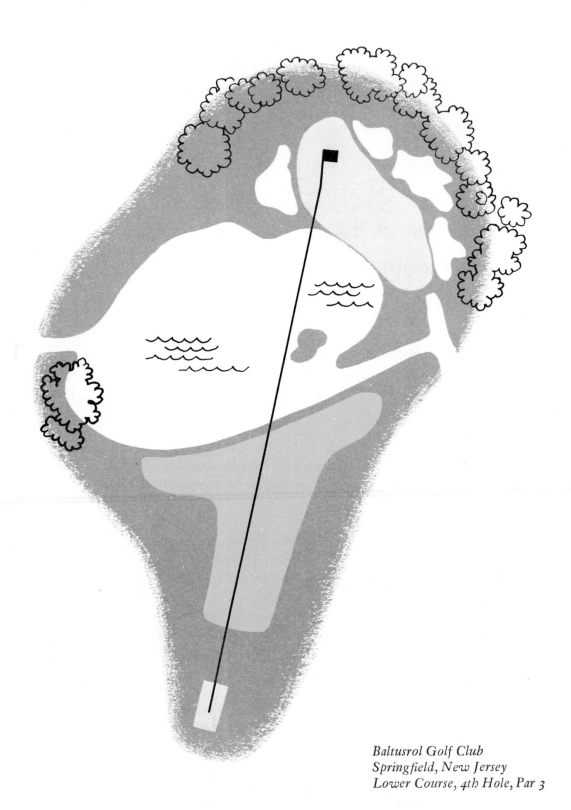

Baltusrol Golf Club
Springfield, New Jersey
Lower Course, 4th Hole, Par 3

Aerial view of green.

Bobby Jones in a thirty-six-hole playoff for that championship, was the golf professional there for four decades, replacing George Low, father of the fabulous putter man.

I played in the 1954 Open at Baltusrol as an amateur but missed the cut. I did quite a bit better in 1967, when I battled Jack Nicklaus to the wire only to lose as he set a new Open record of 275. I shot 279.

It was here in 1967 that Lee Trevino first gained national fame. It was the most significant single thing in Trevino's career up to that time, when he finished fifth and won six thousand dollars. It staked him with money he needed to stay on tour, and he scored his first Open triumph the following year at Oak Hill in Rochester, New York.

I had arranged with Lee to return to Baltusrol to play the fourth hole with me. While we were there, I got him reminiscing about that trip from Texas in 1967 to try his luck.

"It was actually my second Open, but what a lot of people don't know is that I came here with four hundred dollars in my pocket, three pairs of slacks, four shirts, one pair of golf shoes, and twelve clubs. If you remember,

Marty Fleckman was leading going into the last day, and I don't even remember who I was paired with.

"I birdied the tenth hole and they put my name up on the leader board. It was the first time I ever learned how to spell my name correctly.

"I yelled, 'Look' and got to choking, three-putting twelve and fourteen, but I still finished fifth. What can I say? It's where my life began.

"I stayed in a motel right close to here, and you know, I didn't have a sport coat. I didn't know when you came east of the Mississippi you had to have a lot of clothes. They wouldn't let me in the restaurant without a tie or anything.

"So I had to eat in a Chinese restaurant up here. After eating Chinese food for a week, my wife didn't recognize me—my eyes were kinda slanted up.

"Now it's seven years later and over a million dollars. I've only won nineteen tournaments, but four of them were majors. It's just been fantastic.

"It keeps getting tougher to win. Remember, you and I were eighteen under par at Hartford and we tied for second. We got to find new jobs. You can be an airplane pilot and I go back to selling tamales on the street. The year before I was fifteen under par and won the same tournament. I can't keep improving three shots a year.

"But getting back to Baltusrol and that six thousand dollars, it was a bonanza for me. I was making seventy dollars a week working at a driving range. I tell you, only in America can you do what I did."

Trevino was happy to return to Baltusrol. You never forget where it all began. That's why I have a crush on the Masters—it was my first big breakthrough in 1958.

Baltusrol, like all old courses, has greens that are on the same level as the fairways, since they didn't have big equipment available in the old days. The horses and mules graded everything. It is easier to tell which way the greens break just by looking at the surrounding terrain.

The fourth hole is virtually a full carry over water, since the teeing ground runs back from one side of the pond and the green starts at the edge of the other side. The bank at the green is a stone wall.

The large green is oval in shape, except where it narrows to the right side and is two-leveled, the break almost diagonally across the green. The green slopes slightly toward the pond in its entirety.

Three traps guard almost the entire back of the green, and another sits on the left side just beyond the water. A creek carries water off the pond and is close enough off the right edge of the green to catch sliced or pushed tee shots.

118

Lee Trevino and Arnold Palmer practice putting, with Baltusrol clubhouse in background.

When Robert Trent Jones did some rebuilding of the course prior to the 1954 Open championship, he played the course with three club officials. The officials were claiming he made the fourth hole too difficult. So Jones proceeded to make a hole-in-one there that day.

The hole is one of the most beautiful in the country. Besides the water, the stone wall, the creek, and the bunkers, it is framed with dogwood and oak trees behind the green covering the rising landscape.

The day Trevino and I returned to Baltusrol, it was balmy, with very little wind. Trevino played first and, without teeing up the ball, hit a four-iron about twenty feet to the right of the hole in perfect position. He did this after announcing he was going to "make a quick two, grab his money, and run."

119

Lee Trevino and Arnold Palmer before playing hole.

I hit a four-iron, too, but mine was left of the pin and behind it by about twenty-five feet. I couldn't take a good run at a birdie and settled for a tap-in par. Trevino, good as his word, holed his putt for a birdie.

For our low handicapper, club selection is the most important thing in playing this hole. The green is a large one—I would estimate ten thousand square feet—so it is a big target. The low handicapper should aim for the middle or fat part and let it fly with a long iron. With this in mind, he needs two putts for a par and could get lucky and make a birdie.

However, if he doesn't take enough club, he's in the water. If the shot is too long, he's in one of those bunkers and has a difficult shot to the pin.

The middle handicapper has a chance here to make par or even a birdie, particularly if the pin is tucked in on the right front of the green. It is a perfect target for our middle man's slice. If he connects with his driver, starting the ball well to the left, the banana ball will nestle somewhere in the vicinity of the right front of the green.

It is important that our middle man ignore the expanse of water confronting him and just takes a nice, smooth swing. The result is usually a shot of something approaching two hundred yards long that puts him in impressive position on one of the world's greatest par-threes.

When you think about the water carry demanded by the fourth hole, you must realize that our high handicapper is in for a bad time. The chances are that he cannot carry the water from the tee to the putting surface with his best tee shot. Even if he has a dozen free golf balls, our high man is smart to go a different direction than the shortest distance between two points, playing the ball to the right into the rough short of the creek and approaching the green from there. That's all heavy rough there, and it will probably take him four or five shots to get on the green. A double or triple bogey is about the most we can expect of him there.

Before we said good-bye to Baltusrol, I asked Trevino about his businesses and outside interests. I have been traveling the tour for nineteen years and know that my busy life has taken its toll physically and mentally.

"People don't realize," Trevino responded, "that every time you are in town, all those people want is for you to win that week. But that's the price of being a superstar.

Lee Trevino putts as Palmer watches.

View of hole from behind green with clubhouse in background.

"I don't have as many things going as you do, but I have quite a few. And while I'm making business trips and going to banquets and things like that, those young guys are out there hitting golf balls and practicing. Once they become great golfers, they'll find out what it means to train yourself to be a superstar. The money is outside golf, really. What with ventures, joint ventures, developing, building golf courses, golf clubs, golf balls, doing different things—that's where you get rich.

"That's the thing that keeps a guy going. When you say you aren't playing well, people don't understand. They figure you should practice and forget about the outside interests. They should quit their business and just play golf and realize what they are asking.

"When you have as many people dependent on you as I have, you got to take all you can get. Why, if I get the flu or pneumonia, thirteen people are out of work for a week."

Winged Foot Golf Club

MAMARONECK, NEW YORK

WEST COURSE,
10th HOLE, 193 YARDS, PAR 3

Winged Foot has been the site of three U. S. Open championships—
1929, 1959, and 1974. It is one of the older and larger clubs in the world, its
650 members playing something like 20,000 rounds a year on two courses in
New York's Westchester County.

Under the tutelage of Claude Harmon, many young pros have started
their careers there, including Dave Marr, Jack Burke, and Mike Souchak.
Souchak, incidentally, had a chance to win the 1959 Open there but faltered
on the last nine.

The hole is extremely well guarded, with a very narrow opening between traps that spread like half moons around the sides of the green, which
widens and rises to the back.

Out-of-bounds stakes are just six yards behind the green, and a hooked
tee shot that eludes the left trap rolls down a slope into trees.

The green has suffered sinking spells now and again, and that has added
to the difficulty of the putting surface, adding undulations to the already
low front.

A three-iron is the club most used here, and I find the hole an exacting
one. If the pin is back, par is about the best that can be done. In front, you

have a chance to score a birdie if you can elude the traps and keep the ball on the front portion of the green.

Our low handicapper will probably hit a two-iron, but his chances of survival are small. He would be better off with a smooth four-wood, rooting for a par instead of chancing a double bogey with an errant tee shot.

Our middle handicapper, with the usual slice with his driver, is either on the putting surface or chipping or blasting from the sand to the right for a try at a par. More likely it's a bogey.

Our high handicapper can get on this green in two, and with two putts makes a bogey—not an unusual score on this hole.

Princeville

KAUAI, HAWAII

OCEAN NINE, 7th HOLE, 200 YARDS, PAR 3

I have played quite a bit of golf in Hawaii and have found such courses as Waialae and Royal Kaanapali to be excellent tests of golf. I am involved myself in several new courses being created on the interesting terrain of the Islands. But to add a touch of variety to this compilation of great holes, I decided to defer to the opinion of my friend Dave Marr, who has spent quite a bit more time than I have in Hawaii. He had a quick and positive response.

"One of the finest holes I've ever seen is the seventh hole on the Ocean nine in Princeville on the island of Kauai. It has everything that a championship hole needs, and there is also a place for the high handicapper and the ladies.

"First of all, it may be the prettiest hole in the world, since the ocean is on the right, trees and foliage on the left, mountains in the background; it just takes your breath away.

"It also takes your desire to play away some days when the wind is blowing because you must carry the ocean to reach the green in one.

"There are days when a six-iron is sufficient with the wind behind you, but that is only 5 per cent of the time. The rest of the time, we never use the back tee because it is too long a carry.

"From the middle championship tee, I use either a three-iron or four-wood, depending on pin placement. The green is set so that the narrow part faces you and the length is from your left to right. On the left, it is a shorter shot.

"Low handicappers have no difficulty with the hole, as they usually hook the ball and hit it far enough. The question is how close they get to the pin on an undulating green.

"A middle handicapper has trouble, since the ocean is on his bad side— the right. He must spank a driver over the foliage and hope he can carry 180 yards from the front tee. It's a sometimes thing, mostly sometimes no.

"There is a tee for the high handicapper far to the left of the championship and middle tees. It is around the foliage, and the only trouble is way right to the ocean. A high handicapper can almost reach the green from here and make a birdie or a par.

"In fact, both my boys made their first pars here. And, one day, I made my all-time high. Quite a hole."

Oak Hill Country Club

ROCHESTER, NEW YORK

11th HOLE, 192 YARDS, PAR 3

Oak Hill has hosted the U. S. Open twice—in 1956 and in 1968.

In '56 I was still in contention in the final round when I came to the eleventh hole; then hit the ball in the water and wound up with a six. It was at the eleventh in 1968 that Lee Trevino started his charge in the final round to beat Bert Yancey. Trevino's birdie two and another birdie on twelve clinched the championship.

The par-three is half guarded by water, and there is a willow tree that reaches out to catch an errant shot and drop it in the water. A long iron must be threaded through the tall trees, and all faded shots will catch the water. Pin placement on this hole is a key, as the pin is usually tucked on the right, where it takes a magnificently hit shot to get close.

I hit a three-iron there most of the time, and it is the correct stick if struck properly.

Our low handicapper will probably go at it with a two-iron to make sure he carries the water and the finger of sand that loops in front of the green. However, there is one thing wrong with that strategy. If he hits the two-iron solidly, the ball will carry the green and land in a yawning bunker beyond the putting surface. It is a difficult hole for the low handicapper, and an average score in ten rounds would be a bogey-four.

127

Our middle handicapper has a chance to hit his slice with a driver or three-wood, depending on his distance capabilities. The shot has a chance to reach the green and set up a three. His lack of distance gives him a plus on this hole.

Our high handicapper is in trouble as usual, for anywhere there is water, he is in trouble. However, after laying up with a five-iron, he has a simple wedge over the water. Of course, for our high man, nothing is simple. His best score is four; his worst, about any number.

Preston Trail Golf Club

DALLAS, TEXAS

11th HOLE, 183 YARDS, PAR 3

For years Dallas took a back seat to the charisma of Jack Burke and Jimmy Demaret with their Champions Club in Houston and to the famed Colonial Country Club in Fort Worth and Ben Hogan's long-time association with the Colonial National Invitational Tournament. At first, the Dallas Open couldn't even get a date in the spring schedule when the other two events were played.

Then, in 1968, the Salesmanship Club of Dallas moved the tournament to the new and exclusive Preston Trail Golf Club, boosted the prize money, and named the tournament after one of its members, Byron Nelson, who lives nearby. It is now one of the premier stops on the tour. Preston Trail is an all-men's club, with a membership roster that identifies with much of the wealth in Texas.

The eleventh hole, a good, middle-distance par-three, is one of six on the course affected by the presence of White Rock Creek, which flows from one end of the course to the other. Ponds bring water into play on three or four other holes.

The tee for the eleventh is elevated and located in a chute on trees. The shot must carry water within ten feet of the front edge of the green. Bunkers guard the front of the green left and right, with another farther back on the right. The creek meanders along that right side but pretty much out of play. Trees are close by the left side. The green rises toward the back, so that any shot over the green requires a return pitch onto a downslope—tough indeed.

The club at the eleventh can be anything from a four- to a six-iron, with the wind almost always a factor in club selection, as is typical in Texas. The water really doesn't present a big problem for the pros, but it catches many a golf ball struck by our middle and high handicappers.

I had a good shot at a Nelson title in 1970 when, for the third time that year, I faced a thirty-six-hole finale of a tournament in which I was in strong contention. Jack Nicklaus and I battled head to head through those last thirty-six holes with John Schroeder, the third member of the group on that long day. Schroeder held up well in the situation and finished just a shot off the pace.

My par and a scrambling bogey by Nicklaus at the eighteenth set up a playoff, which started at the par-five fifteenth. Jack really nailed his tee shot and was hole high in the fringe in two. I did not catch my drive and couldn't even get home when I used my driver from a rather tight lie. Nicklaus got down easily in two and won when I missed my birdie putt from about twelve feet.

Medinah Country Club, Medinah, Illinois—No. 3 Course, 2nd hole.
Arnold Palmer tees off.

Baltusrol Golf Club, Springfield, New Jersey—Lower Course, 4th hole. View of green from far to golfer's right.

Firestone Country Club, Akron, Ohio—South Course, 16th hole. View from fairway toward green.

Augusta National Golf Club, Augusta, Georgia — 13th hole. View toward green from golfer's right rough.

Seminole Golf Club, Palm Beach, Florida—15th hole. Aerial of hole as it would be played the "safe way" to golfer's left. Arnold Palmer and Laura Baugh played it across water and to right of cluster of trees.

Cherry Hills Country Club,
Denver, Colorado—17th hole.
Aerial from behind island green.

Olympic Club, San Francisco, California—Lake Course, 16th hole. Aerial view showing heavily-populated San Francisco suburban area.

Whitemarsh Valley Country Club

LAFAYETTE HILL, PENNSYLVANIA

9th HOLE, 125 YARDS, PAR 3

I didn't realize it at the time, but after I had completed my list of golf holes to be included in this book, it occurred to me that the two shortest holes of the entire fifty-four holes I picked are both located in Philadelphia.

The thirteenth at Merion, which I selected among my "best eighteen" holes, measures only 129 yards. Even at that, it is four yards longer than my other Philadelphia par-three—the ninth hole at Whitemarsh Valley Country Club, which has hosted a variously named and backed tournament in the Pennsylvania city since 1963.

Like Merion's thirteenth, the short ninth at Whitemarsh extracts a lot of bogeys, mainly because there is very little margin for error. Trees and out of bounds are close by to the right and at the base of the abrupt slope behind the green; the terrain also drifts away toward the clubhouse to the left; the green is virtually encircled with traps—all in all, an interesting nine-iron or wedge tee shot that had better land on the putting surface.

Whitemarsh, in general, is a tight course, and the ninth hole presents its risks at a crucial point in the round, either sending you optimistically to the back nine or ruining a decent front nine. A birdie at the ninth in the final round of the 1967 tournament sustained a charge Dan Sikes had mounted, and he went on to a winning 267 that tied the tournament record.

That first tour tournament at Whitemarsh was quite memorable for me. It was my seventh and last U.S. victory that year, and its twenty-six-thousand-dollar first prize assured me of finishing as the year's No. 1 money winner.

Because the tournament that first year had to be scheduled in early October, following events in Seattle and Portland, our officials granted the dates only after the sponsors agreed to provide airline passage for all players coming East to Philadelphia and going back West to Las Vegas for the Sahara.

You know, that first-place check might have been as much as fifty thousand dollars even back in those days if the sponsors had not elected to pick up all of those air fares.

Hazeltine National Golf Club

CHASKA, MINNESOTA

16th HOLE, 214 YARDS, PAR 3

Ever hear of a dogleg par-three?

Hazeltine National Golf Club, out in the Minnesota countryside from Minneapolis, has one—at times. When the pin is set on the extreme left side of the sixteenth hole there, it can't be seen from the tee because of some tall trees down the left side. So it's a one-shot dogleg.

The 1970 U. S. Open championship was played at Hazeltine, and the Robert Trent Jones course stirred up more criticism from the players, particularly Dave Hill, than I had heard in a long time. I certainly wouldn't have gone as far as Hill did ("They ought to plow it up and start all over again"), but I did agree that Hazeltine had some poor holes. Even with the oddity of the imaginary dogleg, the sixteenth is one of Hazeltine's best holes, though.

Gary Player, whose difficulties in the windblown Open at Hazeltine were similar to mine and those of Jack Nicklaus, describes the sixteenth hole this way: "A beautiful hole for the gallery but not for the player. Only a few small trees separate the green from Lake Hazeltine on the right side, and a hogback in the middle of the green can make putting very tricky."

The wind switches around during the day, definitely affecting the play of the hole and the club selection on the tee.

Tony Jacklin, who struck gold at Hazeltine by winning that Open, handled the sixteenth better than most, although he was one over par on it. He hit the green all four days, but he three-putted the first time he played it. Quite a few others in the field would have been well satisfied to have done that well.

It was an unusual Open indeed. Jacklin was just the fourth foreign player to win our Open championship, Harry Vardon, Ted Ray, and Player being the others. Tony is an outstanding player, but still even the greatest of them all just don't win the Open championship by seven strokes going away. The other "name" players were never in serious contention, as virtually everybody except Tony was victimized by horrible windy weather the first day and never got back in the chase. Ironically, the unhappy Hill was really Tony's only challenger, but Dave fired and fell back in the last round.

Westchester Country Club

HARRISON, NEW YORK

1st HOLE, 190 YARDS, PAR 3

The year 1963 was the most peculiar of my big seasons at that point in my career. I won three times on the winter tour, but then had a poor Masters and a much poorer Colonial, where I was also the defending champion. So I forced myself into a four-week layoff, something unheard of for me. I returned for the $100,000 Thunderbird Classic at Westchester Country Club, the second-richest tournament on the tour that year.

That tournament started and ended on the 190-yard first hole—and it launched probably the hottest short stretch of my career. Before the summer was out, I had won the Cleveland and the Western Opens and lost a U. S. Open playoff, then capped it in October by taking the richest 1963 tournament, at Whitemarsh in Philadelphia—a $125,000 purse, $26,000 of it mine for the victory.

It is quite unusual to start a tournament round on a par-three hole. Actually, that Westchester hole is the tenth, but the nines have always been reversed for the Thunderbird and its successor, the Westchester Classic, primarily for the benefit of the galleries.

In any event, that hole is rather innocuous in appearance, usually described as a "routine" par-three. But it is no cinch hole for the three- or four-iron tee shot. If you don't have enough club, you land in a bunker in

135

front of the green. If you pull the shot, a trap at the left probably will catch the ball. If you are long, you have a tough pitch back to a green sloping away from you. A pushed shot is out of bounds. Beware, middle handicapper.

Ask Paul Harney about the hole. Paul, a great guy who actually had his greatest success as a semiregular after taking a good club job at Pleasant Valley in Massachusetts, wound up on that first tee with me at the end of that 1963 Thunderbird. We had tied with 277s and were starting a playoff. I had muffed a fairly short putt on the eighteenth green to bring about the playoff and remarked afterward about it: "I finally found my choking price."

Harney knocked his tee shot over the back left edge of the green and faced the tricky return route. With Paul in that position, I played for the front level of the green to stay below the hole. Harney could not get close with his pitch, missed his putt, and I won with my two for the par.

Perhaps the most memorable Westchester Classic was in 1967, when the tournament started on a Thursday and finished the following Wednesday, with rain and more rain in between. Jack Nicklaus eventually won, but the interesting story involved Dan Sikes. Twice, before rounds in progress were washed out, Sikes was on his way out of town after early poor finishes, got word of the cancellations in time to stick around, and wound up second with a $30,000 check.

Columbus Country Club

COLUMBUS, OHIO

17th HOLE, 219 YARDS, PAR 3

Bobby Nichols is one of my favorite players on the tour. He tees it up, plays as hard as he can, never complains, and goes on and on. He has been a club professional at Firestone for the past few years and seems to play as much now as he ever did. It might be the best job in the country.

Bobby won the PGA championship at the Columbus Country Club in 1964, beating a couple of fellows named Jack Nicklaus and Arnold Palmer, who finished together in second place, three strokes back.

I'm not trying to take anything away from Bobby's win when I say that he had the most adventurous round of his life on the third day at Columbus. People who were catching occasional glimpses of Bobby's round had to think he was shooting somewhere in the eighties. He was all over the course. But the name of the game is not how but how many.

Coming to the seventeenth hole in that third round, Nichols had the lead but was shaky.

The hole is a good par-three, with trees on the right side and a green that is well bunkered. Bobby did something with his tee shot that you rarely see a good player do. He half-shanked a two-iron some seventy yards off line and deep in the woods.

Nichols disappeared into the forest, and it looked like a bogey or double bogey was forthcoming. But Bobby calmly selected his wedge, lofted the ball over the trees, and it hit the pin, almost going in for a two. The next day, just to make sure that the seventeenth was his, Nichols holed a fifty-one-foot birdie putt to end any challenge.

Short Quiz

QUESTION: Who was the first player in a major championship to shoot four rounds under seventy and not win?

ANSWER: No, not Lee Trevino. Remember, he won. Arnold Palmer at Columbus Country Club in the 1964 PGA championship. He shot rounds of 68-68-69-69 and lost to Bobby Nichols by three strokes.

Desert Inn Country Club

LAS VEGAS, NEVADA

16th HOLE, 177 YARDS, PAR 3

I have been going to Las Vegas for some twenty years to play golf and enjoy the nightlife atmosphere of the glittering Nevada city. I have done rather well in the tournaments played there, particularly in the Tournament of Champions at Desert Inn Country Club.

It wasn't until 1962 that I won my first of three championships there, holing from off the back fringe of the final green to nip Billy Casper. But the 1959 tournament was memorable, if not overly successful, and it led me to include the par-three sixteenth hole in this compilation.

I arrived in Las Vegas that year as a recognized contender, for the first time, really. I had won the Masters the year before and several other tournaments since then. I was starting to feel my oats. Unfortunately, I didn't live up to my billing.

I was trying to get something going in the third round when the par-five fifteenth hole killed me with a shot in the water and four putts on the green. For the first time in her life, my wife, Winnie, gave up and headed for the clubhouse.

The sixteenth hole at the Desert Inn is a good par-three of medium range, not overly difficult but interesting, with a pond in front of the green. The trees to the right prevent you from hitting the ball with a draw into the prevailing wind. Instead, you must hit the ball straight or fade it, and that means crossing the water in front of the green. The water continues off to the right, catching a fade that becomes a slice. It can be serious trouble for both our middle and our high handicapper, who are destined for water-logged penalty strokes.

I was laughing on the outside as I left the fifteenth green that day, not really too upset over the disaster at fifteen. I had not been too close anyway. But I have pride in my game and decided to see what I could do about finishing with a couple of birdies on the final three holes.

I selected a six-iron for the shot, and the ball went right in the hole for a one. It was my first ace in competition and one of the few shots that my wife has not seen me play when she was at a tournament. I have made eight aces in all, the other tournament one on tour at Pensacola in 1965.

Quail Hollow Country Club

17th HOLE, 190 YARDS, PAR 3

In 1971 at the Kemper Open in Charlotte, I was paired with Tom Weiskopf on the last day. It seemed we were both out of contention playing through the back nine when, all of a sudden, Tom got hot.

I never saw such putting. On the fifteenth and sixteenth holes, he sank ten-footers for birdies and came to the seventeenth only two strokes off the pace set by three men—Gary Player, Lee Trevino, and Dale Douglass. Weiskopf was charged up now.

The seventeenth is a picturesque par-three and demands a two- or a three-iron. The tee shot has to carry 130 yards over an arm of the course's largest lake and miss two huge sand bunkers on the left side of the green and another at the right front.

There is a bunker in the back to catch a long shot, and the green is also protected by trees and a mound on the right. It is not the kind of hole that you want to play when you need a birdie to play catch-up. And it's certainly not a hole our high handicapper ever wants to play. He has too much water to carry.

Weiskopf's three-iron was a super shot and came to rest about seven feet from the pin. He holed it for a birdie. It was a most difficult shot under pressure and the one that I think won the tournament for him. From there, he went on to birdie eighteen to join a four-way playoff, which began at the fifteenth hole. Tom made his fifth straight birdie on that first extra hole, took home the title, and deserved it. Very few players have ever finished the last round of a tournament so strongly.

The seventeenth was the key, however. To show how tough it is, one hundred thousand dollars was offered for any hole-in-one during the last two rounds. Nobody collected.

Sedgefield Country Club

GREENSBORO, NORTH CAROLINA

16th HOLE, 225 YARDS, PAR 3

One of the things that all of us on the golf tour have found to be generally true is the extra dimension of difficulty we face when we are playing in a tournament in our home area or a place where we have special ties. I guess a fellow tends to try a little harder when he knows a lot of relatives and friends are on hand rooting for him. He probably tries too hard, in fact.

This has happened to me in my native western Pennsylvania (except when I had the help of a partner like Jack Nicklaus a couple of years in the National Team championship), and it's been that way, too, in Greensboro, North Carolina, where I have never won the venerable Greater Greensboro Open. I went to college not far from Greensboro (Wake Forest), and North Carolina has had a special place in my heart ever since. I have made friends there who have been loyal and good ones throughout my career.

I should have won the GGO in 1972, but maybe I didn't use my head at one point. Well, that's not exactly right. Perhaps it was more that I decided to play a shot the way people expect Arnold Palmer to play it. And I guess I would play it the same way today in the same situation. Which was—

Because of a rain-out, we were finishing the tournament with a thirty-six-hole Sunday at Sedgefield Country Club. As I stood on the sixteenth tee that afternoon, waiting for the back-up ahead of me to clear, I had a two-stroke lead with three holes to play. The sixteenth is a rugged par-three—long at 225 yards although downhill, with a green guarded front, left, and right by a water hazard, and traps right front and left rear—in short, nothing but trouble.

In normal weather, a two-iron is the club, but I felt I needed a wood that day. Of course, I could have laid up, pitched on, and tried for my par that way. I know some people thought I should have done this, but, really, that's not my style, my game. Besides, two strokes—or the one shot I was more likely to retain playing it that way—can disappear fast on the tour. No, I am a great believer in not changing tactics. I've won tournaments being bold and lost some being bold. I always expect to execute the necessary shot.

In any event, I let fly with my three-wood and hooked it into the creek. I thought I could get it out of the creek and I did, but I left the ball in a bare lie with the bunker between me and the green. I was beginning to lose my composure as I dumped the next shot into the sand, blasted out, and two-putted for a six. Pars at the last two holes left me a stroke behind and my best chance ever to win at Greensboro down the drain.

Obviously, the top amateurs will play the sixteenth the same way as I did and will often get the same results as I did that day. Our less able players won't even have to think about it. They'll try the lay-up shot, the pitch, and likely make a four or a five on the hole.

An interesting thing about that day at Greensboro: That was the first tournament in which I wore contact lenses. Surprisingly, they didn't bother me very much even being in my eyes so long that day. Perhaps, if I hadn't encountered that disaster at the sixteenth, I might never have gone to glasses on the golf course.

I wasn't the only player to be manhandled by the sixteenth hole that day. When I lost those strokes, it set up a first-place tie between George Archer and Tommy Aaron and a playoff. Aaron lost—by hooking his tee shot on the sixteenth hole into the same creek.

Pleasant Valley Country Club

SUTTON, MASSACHUSETTS

16th HOLE, 183 YARDS, PAR 3

There has been some good news and some bad news for me on the testing, par-three sixteenth hole at Pleasant Valley Country Club, one of New England's newer, better, and certainly busiest national tournament courses.

Pleasant Valley was the scene almost annually for a decade starting in the mid-1960s of tournaments on both the PGA and LPGA tours, drawing huge, golf-starved crowds from the heavily populated areas of eastern Massachusetts and other nearby states. (Nowhere else do both tours play the same course the same season.) The last major championship in New England was the Open at Brookline in 1963.

I won once at Pleasant Valley and had a near miss another time; hence the good news-bad news.

In 1968, I won the only Kemper Open played at Pleasant Valley before it was moved to Charlotte, North Carolina. I made a comforting par on the sixteenth, which presents you with a tee shot to a green sitting far below you, sloping forward, long and narrow, well cushioned with bunkers. That par made my victory relatively easy.

Pleasant Valley emerged on the men's tour in 1965 when it hosted the second Carling World Open, a since-departed giant of a tournament of international proportions. It featured the biggest purse in golf up to that time:

two hundred thousand dollars. I was chasing the late Tony Lema down the stretch in that tournament. I finally caught Tony at the fifteenth hole and felt I had a good chance to keep it going and win the tournament.

But my tee shot—a six-iron, as I recall—flew just a little bit too far right, and I missed the green. This is usually fatal on this hole. I chipped weakly from the right rough, left myself a difficult putt, and took a bogey. It was fatal as Tony went on to beat me by two strokes.

That the hole is tough is evident because in that tournament it was picked to carry a one-hundred-thousand-dollar bonus for a hole-in-one. It used to be about 220 yards but was changed for the better to about 180, still a most difficult hole.

A funny incident happened to me on this course as I was about to win that Kemper Open in 1968.

On the eighteenth hole, I put my approach in a bunker. A fan jumped in the sand, picked my ball up, and threw it on the green. I had to drop the ball back in the same spot in the bunker and got a bad lie. However, all's well that ends well. I blasted to within eight inches of the cup.

Par Fives

Usually I like a par-five hole that gives you a chance to go for the green on your second shot. That way, if a player pulls off a good shot, he has a chance to gain two strokes on par and should get at least a birdie if he reaches the putting surface in two.

But when I started to pick the par-five holes that impressed me, I wound up with some that could not be reached in two. Perhaps my memories of the holes swayed my opinion. I have tried to decide which ones I would like to play over and over again.

Obviously, some of my par-fives are just that, at best, for all but the strong players. Yet I think that is only fair, since power is a big factor in good golf.

So let's see what we have for you in the way of par-fives.

Firestone Country Club

AKRON, OHIO

SOUTH COURSE,
16th HOLE, 625 YARDS, PAR 5

The sixteenth hole at Firestone brings back memories to me. Memories? Nightmares, I mean. The first hole dubbed "The Monster" by the players, it is exactly that.

It has everything mean and nasty. Bunkers, ditches, trees, water—you name it—everything that's troublesome, plus a green that is so hard the ball winces when it lands. It is a hole that is wisely played for a par and dangerous to play for a birdie.

And it can do a contender in, as it did me in 1960. I had won the Masters and U. S. Open, finished second in the British Open, and arrived at Firestone with a good chance to win three of the Big Four and accomplish something else that has never been done: win an American Grand Slam of the Masters, Open, and PGA.

Coming to the sixteenth hole during the third round, I was in the chase. Then the course got to me. I drove the ball into the right bunker—the second of two—located strategically on the high side of the fairway. The fairway slopes quickly to the left, so you must keep the ball as high as possible yet try to avoid the bunkers.

I went too far to the right, though, and put the ball in the sand. The lie was good and, knowing that the hole is 625 yards, I decided to go with a

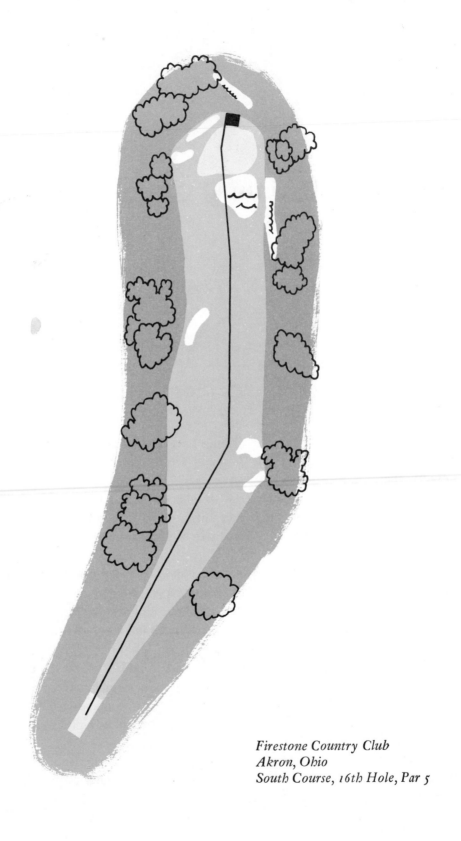

Firestone Country Club
Akron, Ohio
South Course, 16th Hole, Par 5

four-wood. I wanted to place myself in position for a wedge or a nine-iron shot into the green so I could go for a birdie. All I had to do was hit the ball straight ahead, and the downhill terrain would take care of the rest.

Somewhere along the backswing, all my strategy went into the ash can. The trees that lined the right side of the fairway beyond the bunkers stood there blithely as my four-wood shot sailed over them and into the rough of the woods. I was petrified. Now I was in jail.

When I studied the situation, I saw an opening through which, if I could hit the shot accurately, I could put the ball on the green. In those days, trouble shots were sort of down my alley, so I elected to go for it. But the ball ticked a branch and dropped into the ditch that parallels the fairway just short of the pond in front of the green. I couldn't play that shot, dropped out with a one-stroke penalty, knocked the ball on the green, and three-putted. That added up to eight strokes and took me out of the chase for the championship, particularly when I proceeded to bogey the last two holes. I have been chasing that title in vain every year since.

Oddly enough, I hit the green in two strokes in the 1963 American Golf Classic and so did Bobby Nichols, who is the professional at Firestone and the man with whom I played the hole in putting this chapter together.

Remember that the fairway bends sharply to the left and is downhill, so

View down fairway from crest of hill.

anything left of center winds up in the rough, or worse, in the woods. In fact, a smart player should hit a three- or four-wood straightaway and forget about the length. Yet if you go at the green with much more than a wedge, it is almost impossible to stop the ball on the front half of the green. We pros figure you must birdie the par-fives, but "The Monster" should really be played for five.

On the day Bobby and I played the hole, there was a little breeze in our faces and we both hit drives short of and below the two bunkers on the right. I hit a three-wood, Bobby hit a one-iron, and we were both in good position for wedge shots to the green from just outside a hundred yards. This is one situation in which you can get too close to the green. I know that sounds absurd, but when you have water right up to the edge of the putting surface, pitching is difficult. It is better to hit a full wedge from a hundred yards or so that plops on the green with plenty of bite. Shorter shots over hazards are harder to gauge and don't have as much action.

We both zeroed in pretty well with our wedges, striking the green short of the hole, which you have to do to have a reasonable putt for a birdie. Bobby missed his, but I got mine in, cutting that 1960 score on the hole in half. Wouldn't that have been nice in the long ago.

Aerial toward green showing position of lake in front of green.

Arnold Palmer (right) and Bobby Nichols prepare to play shots to green.

When you see playing professionals with cool putters contented with pars at the sixteenth, why then should a low handicapper expect a birdie? The length of the drive is not of great importance. A three-wood off the tee and a three-wood second shot put the low handicapper in position to hit something around a seven- or eight-iron to the green. The pin is usually tucked up toward the front on the right, and the water to the back right comes into play if you are coming in from far to the left side of the fairway.

Our low handicapper should be satisfied with a par the same as the professionals. Five is a good score on this hole—a par-five that is a genuine par-five, with little margin for error. Of course, it's primarily a one-shot hole for the low man as well as the professionals—that delicate third shot.

The medium handicapper should be able to play this hole for six, and possibly five, slice or no slice, just so he doesn't hook the ball on the first two shots. A good tee shot will leave him short of the bunkers. Two more full shots will put him in position short of the pond for his short-iron approach to the green.

Most middle handicappers can play the approach shot and can putt

Bobby Nichols tees off.

reasonably well. That is what separates them from the high boys, who have not mastered any shot fully. Depending on his approach, our middle man should have a putt for a par and a likely six, which, after all, is only one shot higher than the pros usually make on the hole.

Our high handicapper will do well to finish this hole. His drive probably won't clear the hill from the back tee, and there is no margin for error, left or right. It may take him at least five shots to get in the vicinity of the water. If he tries to go over the pond, I wish him luck. He will be better off if he plays to the left of the water and chips on the green from there, probably in seven. If he doesn't three-putt, he avoids double figures anyway.

A much lower handicapper had an eight there once.

154

Augusta National Golf Club

AUGUSTA, GEORGIA

13th HOLE, 475 YARDS, PAR 5

Now we return to Augusta National Golf Club, where I made my only selection of more than one hole among my "best eighteen."

You can well imagine why I have a little extra feeling for Augusta National. Winning the prestigious Masters championship four times there has something to do with it. But I don't think I really have to go to great pains to justify selection of two holes at Augusta, since just about everybody I know rates Augusta National as one of the world's great courses, embodying many outstanding holes.

The superb par-three twelfth was my first choice. Then, when I thought about it, I knew that the par-five thirteenth also had to be in the group. The two go together like Frick and Frack. To play the twelfth and skip the thirteenth would be like calling off the Super Bowl at halftime. The two holes seem to play as a single unit.

If, by chance, you have birdied the twelfth, you step onto the thirteenth tee exhilarated. In that state, the long expanse of fairway, with its slight dogleg to the left, seems to be inviting you to come ahead and make another birdie—or even an eagle.

If you have parred the twelfth, a satisfactory development for anybody on that tough hole, the thirteenth seems to be more of a challenge. You notice more that the fairway narrows at the dogleg, with the woods and creek to the left watching over it like a mama cat over newborn kittens. You realize, too, that you don't want to stray to the right, lengthening your second shot and risking the interference of the small patch of trees on that side of the dogleg. You know that the best move is a straightaway drive, avoiding the trouble and keeping the green within range of a good second shot.

However, if you have just made a bogey or double bogey (not an infrequent occurrence), the thirteenth hole looks like the ogre it really is. Even the number 13 seems to be flashing the warning of bad luck. The fairway seems nonexistent on the left side, and the tournament gallery on the right, or safe side, appears to have pushed forward, further narrowing the fairway in the mind's eye. After the setback at twelve, you are determined to get a birdie at thirteen so you can get back in the chase quickly. This is not always the wisest approach to the hole. A hurried or pulled tee shot can lead to another bogey or double bogey and destroy you as a contender.

The urge to hit the ball hard and around the corner is a compelling one but, here again, patience is best. A fairly well hit tee shot will give you enough distance to go for the green in two, if the ball is not too far to the right. The closer to the left side, the better to attack the green. In addition to the shorter shot, the left side generally gives you a flatter lie in that fairway, which slopes rather severely toward the creek, leveling off in the final

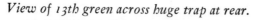

View of 13th green across huge trap at rear.

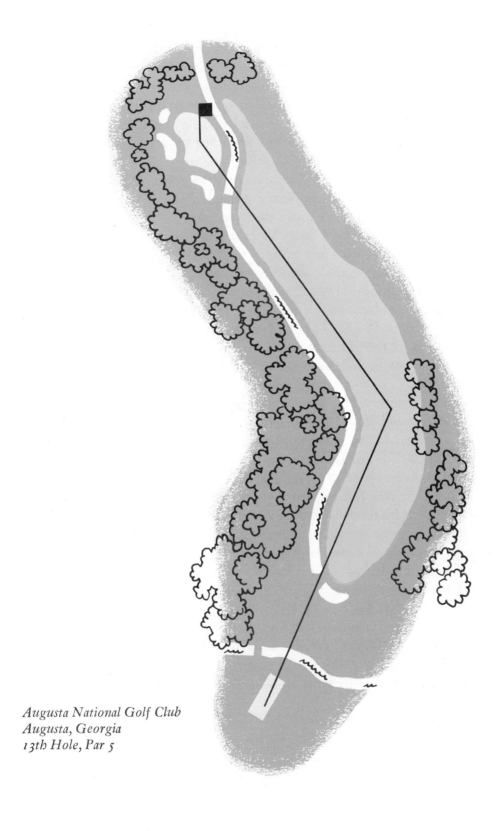

Augusta National Golf Club
Augusta, Georgia
13th Hole, Par 5

yards outside the hazard. The hole measures 475 yards but, if the tee shot goes to the right, it's at least seventy-five to a hundred yards longer. In that case, it's next to impossible to reach the green with the next shot.

The green itself presents problems uncommon to many putting surfaces. It is long—Doc Middlecoff once holed an eighty-six-foot putt that was walked off by a golf writer—and it is protected by water, woods, bunkers, and everything else hazardous to the golfer.

The ditch on the left side disappears near the green, and a creek materializes in front. The creek runs from extreme left all the way around to the back right. Bunkers abound above the green on the left side, which is the safe way home if there is any doubt about the carry of the second shot.

The green slopes from left to right toward the creek, with a ridge just right of center. During the tournament the cup is usually on the right side and rarely in back, since the ball tends to roll once it reaches the green. The most difficult pin placement is front right, which requires a daring shot to get in range for an eagle putt. The golfer must ignore the creek in front and on the right and fly the ball right at the stick—very difficult except for the extremely long hitters, who in the right conditions can be hitting as low as a five-iron.

When I won my first Masters in 1958, I reached the thirteenth green with a three-wood second shot and holed an eighteen-foot putt for an eagle in the final round. This came right on the heels of the embedded-ball incident at the twelfth that I described in the earlier chapter and before I knew I had my three for the twelfth. What a tremendous lift that was.

Most of the pros feel cheated if they do not get a birdie at thirteen, although it is far from simple to do. Even after a perfectly placed tee shot, the second shot must be accurate, and, even if you reach the putting surface, the route to the cup is perilous, to say the least.

There have been many incidents of the thirteenth hole taking its toll or giving a boost to a challenger.

Art Wall birdied it in 1959 and went on to birdie four of the next five holes to win the championship. After making a birdie at twelve on the final day of the 1937 Masters, Byron Nelson was like the guy we talked about earlier. He reached the edge of the thirteenth green in two, chipped in for an eagle, and made up six shots on Ralph Guldahl in two holes, as Guldahl went 5–6.

The bid of Billy Joe Patton, the famed North Carolina amateur, to be the only amateur to win the title ended at the thirteenth hole in 1954. Patton, who was chasing no less than Sam Snead and Ben Hogan in the final

First half of fairway as seen from tee.

*Tommy Aaron hits
fairway shot.*

round, already had registered a hole-in-one and two birdies and was making a mockery of Augusta when he arrived at the thirteenth hole. Even though he had scant chance of reading the green with his second shot, Billy Joe let fly with a four-wood and went into the creek in front of the green. While playing partner Jimmy Demaret looked on in dismay, Patton climbed down to play the shot and failed to get the ball out. He then elected to drop out, made a double bogey, and wound up a single stroke behind the leaders, Snead and Hogan.

It is the classic par-five, one that challenges the player to go for broke, play conservatively, or just play carefully. Some players vow that laying up your second shot short of the creek leaves an easy wedge to set up a birdie putt with none of the risks involved. Of course, most of the players who say this are among the shorter hitters and better wedge players.

That the thirteenth is not invincible is easily proven by the scores in the 1953 tournament. No fewer than thirteen eagles were recorded as Ben Hogan set the then four-round record of 274 strokes (since bettered by Jack Nicklaus in 1965 and by Ray Floyd in 1976 with 271).

I have played the thirteenth hole with varying degrees of success. Actually, it is suited to my game, as I can draw the ball off the tee and get around the corner for a short shot to the green. I haven't played the hole too well in recent years, and that is part of the reason I have not been near the winner's circle for a while at Augusta.

Tommy Aaron and I played the thirteenth as well as the twelfth in the recent visit. En route to his victory in 1973, Tommy played the thirteenth hole in three under par, part of the reason he won the title. In the final round, Tommy had played the front nine in four under par, but bogeyed the tenth and eleventh holes. He managed a par at twelve, and I asked Tommy to describe how he felt when he reached the thirteenth tee.

"Well, Arnie, I had made a good turn. I was four under and feeling pretty good until I bogeyed ten and eleven. I then faced the twelfth hole, a very critical one, and managed a par. It was then I started thinking about birdie once more.

"I remember thinking, 'Well, now, if I can get a good drive here and maybe make a four, and maybe get another birdie going in, I might have a chance.'

"I hit a real good drive, probably a little better than what I had in mind, because I pulled the ball slightly and it went right around the corner. I had a four-iron shot to the green. The other two times I went for the green in the tournament, I had hit a three-wood and a four-wood, so I put some fifty yards extra on that tee shot.

"I made a four there, got back my composure, and went on to realize my lifelong dream of winning the Masters. I'm from Georgia, you know, and winning that green jacket has been my whole life."

It was the same way I felt the first time I realized I had a good chance to win the Masters. There is no way to put the feeling in words—it's like you are on another planet.

Aaron and I both hit big tee shots around the corner (you must remember, we weren't playing a tournament that day, and we let it fly) and were in good position for our second shots. Tommy elected to hit a three-iron—the pin was in that rugged right front position—and he pulled the shot to the left edge of the green.

View of back fairway along creek to dogleg.

I hit a four-iron and also pulled it to the left. We both got down in two. I almost holed my sixty-foot chip over the hump in the green, and Tommy two-putted from forty feet.

There are few low-handicap amateurs who can play this hole the way we played it. Occasionally, a good tee shot will put them in position to try for it but, lacking the consistency bred of constant practice and constant pressure, a well-placed second shot is questionable. I think a low handicapper can get across the creek with two good woods occasionally, but he will rarely be on the putting surface. He will have to either play a bunker shot or a long chip to get in position for a birdie.

A low handicapper who weighs the odds realizes he is better off playing short and relying on his wedge to get him close for a birdie. That way, he eliminates the need for a big tee shot, which could cause creek or wood trouble. A long iron, perhaps even a medium iron, then puts him in place for a wedge pitch to the green. Some prefer a longer wedge shot to a shorter one, as the half shot is one of the most difficult.

The medium handicapper is in trouble here only with his third shot. The tee shot and following three-wood should put him somewhere on the right side of the fairway or slightly in the rough, which is not too bad at that point. Assuming that he has hit his tee shot 180 yards and his second 150 yards, both with slices, he has avoided all the trouble on the hole.

The average medium handicapper with that slicing tendency still has a long iron or wood shot left to the green, since he has come the long way along the right side of the fairway, say, 160 to 180 yards. With his slice, the medium faces a shot where the whole creek comes into play. He must start his wood shot well to the left of the green and root for it to be long enough to carry the creek as it slices toward the hole.

It may be more to his advantage to play the third shot short and depend on a decent pitch shot and a good putt for the par, which eliminates the double or triple bogey facing him if he greedily tries for the green from too far away.

The high handicapper can score anything on this hole above seven. He may even have a problem getting over the ditch between the tee and the fairway, and he may take at least five shots to get where it is possible to cross the creek. It is possible, but the high handicapper rarely crosses a hazard on the first try. The hole is too difficult for our beginner, but he shouldn't get discouraged, just try harder.

Seminole Golf Club

PALM BEACH, FLORIDA

15th HOLE, 517 YARDS, PAR 5

Very few people know that Seminole Golf Club, a quiet playground of Palm Beach society, is one of the best golf courses in the entire world. It is a haven for the affluent and has not had the publicity it deserves, since the few tournaments that have been played there have been amateur events or relatively private pro-amateurs.

Ben Hogan used to sharpen his game at Seminole, first under the guidance of Henry Picard and then under the tutelage of Claude Harmon, perhaps the game's most famous and productive teacher. Harmon is no slouch as a player, either. Consider that Claude won the Masters back in 1948 and, what is even more impressive, scored a sixty here at Seminole, an incredible scoring feat regardless of the competition.

The fifteenth hole at Seminole is the most challenging. The area where the normal drive lands is almost entirely surrounded by water, and the dry land on the left is perilously close to a ditch that runs down the left side of the hole.

The lake in front of the tee is 70 yards wide, and the ball must carry 225 yards from the championship tee to traverse the water and reach the fairway on the other side. Adding to the difficulty of the drive are a couple of pot bunkers and some nasty rough and bushes on the left.

164

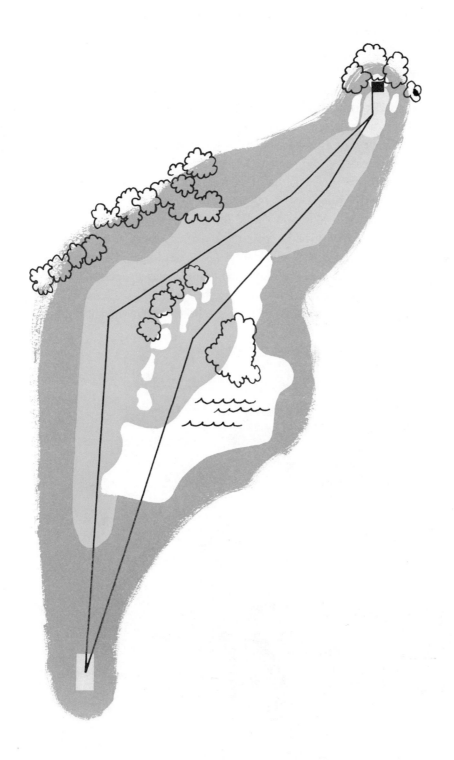

Seminole Golf Club
Palm Beach, Florida
15th Hole, Par 5

When the prevailing wind is blowing, it comes in from about eleven o'clock into the player's face. Reaching the green in two strokes demands a gargantuan effort; in fact, it is nigh impossible into the wind.

The green itself is positioned so that the player sees only the shallow part. It is shaped like a large oval lying from left to right. Three of Seminole's 215 traps protect the green. One guards the left side and another catches errant shots on the right, with still a third behind the green. To add to the difficulty of this particular manicured piece of tropical forest, trees line the right side of the second fairway beyond the second crossing of the water so that any drive right of center eliminates any chance of a second shot reaching the green.

As you can see, it is not a hole on which you expect to make a birdie. However, the day Laura Baugh and I played, there was no wind, the sun was bright, and the ball would carry. I was glad that it was such a nice day because the girl who was my playing opponent was a recent addition to the ladies' professional tour and I was hoping she would do well.

There is an alternate way to play the hole so that the short hitters do not

Laura Baugh in action shot.

Ground-level view toward green.

have to lay up from the tee. It is called "Highway A1A," which is a secondary route that runs the length of Florida along the eastern coastline. You play to the left of the sand traps and up the left side, but there is virtually no chance for a birdie going that roundabout route.

The wind was at our backs rather than coming off the ocean the day Laura and I played, easing the hole considerably. Hitting from the white tees, Laura easily cleared the water and was in "Position A," just left of center. I played the blue tees and hit the ball just to the right of her line and a little behind her ball.

Even on this calm day, I pumped a three-wood as hard as I could and was still short of the green but left with an easy pitch or chip. Laura followed suit with a three-wood and we both wedged within fifteen feet of the hole. I missed my putt but Laura knocked hers in for a birdie.

Let me say this. Anyone who can birdie the fifteenth hole at Seminole has a good career ahead. When you figure that Laura Baugh won the Women's Amateur at sixteen and joined the LPGA tour with considerable early success, you know we should be hearing from her for a long time.

A friend of mine, Mickey Van Gerbig, is a scratch player from the championship tees at Seminole and has played the course steadily since he was a youngster. Mickey is a consistently long hitter who, unless his drive is

View of hole from behind green.

errant, finds the fifteenth at Seminole to his liking. That's because he can handle its length, while most of his fellow low handicappers are in trouble from the blue tees.

The low handicapper has too much pride not to try to carry the water. He wants to play from those championship tees. The fact that he must hit the ball hard usually throws him off track. He swings a little more vigorously than usual and either pulls the ball or pushes it to the right. Since this tee shot demands accuracy as well as distance, the low handicapper is usually in trouble. Even if he does clear the front lake, our low man usually is in bad position for a second shot. He's either in the trees or bunkers on the left or blocked by the trees on the right. It is also possible for him to pull the ball badly enough that it lands in the ditch.

It is almost a predictable bogey or even seven for our low handicapper, since the hole was designed for long, accurate hitters. Few of our low men can consistently drive it both long and where they aim it. However, a good drive sets up the possibility of a birdie, and that's what brings our low man back to the championship tee.

I cannot think of a way that our middle handicapper can play the hole across the water. Even from the white tees, a slice is fatal—it is bound to catch the pond. Our middle man certainly should go the alternate route, which also is fraught with hazards. The ditch will handle anything going to the extreme left, and the trees along the island peninsula will handle anything with a slice. Handle it? I mean ruin it! His best bet is to use a four- or five-wood on his first shot, aiming well to the left of the pond. Hit a short iron so he will not catch the water with his second shot. Use the four-wood again to get across the second pond and hope to get down in three or four, meaning he will have avoided the bunkers and the trees—no easy task.

The high handicapper has to play safe for a seven. I am not trying to be funny when I say this. A double bogey on this hole is a good score for our man, who can play only an occasional decent shot. From the front tee, he hits an iron toward the clearing on the left of the lake. He hits his second shot the same way down the left side and is ready to try a fairway wood for his third, aiming well to the left.

Now he is ready to hit toward the hole as the water is behind, hopefully, and he lies four about 120 yards from the green. His biggest problem now is to get down in three strokes for the good score (for him) of seven. However, if I were a betting man, I would wager our high man will be in double figures on this most treacherous of holes.

Chris Dunphy, the celebrated matchmaker, was the guardian of Seminole for many years. Chris arranged games among the nation's greatest players and personalities and supervised the handicapping so that it came nearest to evaluating the players' games.

Seminole is located among the rolling dunes along the ocean north of Palm Beach, secluded from the traffic flow of U. S. Highway 1, which passes nearby. Hogan usually tuned up for the Masters there. Both Presidents Kennedy and Eisenhower enjoyed playing Seminole. It is another monument to Donald Ross, the famed golf course architect from Scotland, who designed the course in 1929. Ross is the same man who designed Pinehurst No. 2, so he has two courses among the nation's elite.

Arnold Palmer, Laura Baugh in fairway.

Cherry Hills Country Club

DENVER, COLORADO

17th HOLE, 548 YARDS, PAR 5

If I may prevail upon the reader at this point, I would like to reminisce about a weekend in Denver, Colorado, when my childhood dream came true and my career and life caught onto a skyrocket.

I had been on the tour since 1955 and won quite a few golf tournaments, including two Masters championships, yet the jury was still out in 1960. I had not won the Open championship. Yet, when I won at Augusta that April, I said I was determined to win the Grand Slam—the Open, British Open, and PGA along with the Masters, all that year.

I don't blame people for thinking I was nuts. Yet, when you are young, nothing seems impossible and nothing really is, if you can put your mind and your thinking in the right vein. I really thought I could do it and, looking back, I should have. I am not saying this boastfully, but rather with just a little regret. I had every chance in the world, everything going for me.

When I arrived at Denver that June, I was kind of a half celebrity because of the two Masters victories. The birdie-birdie finish that won the Masters for me that year had my spirits and confidence as high as they could be. I was not a youngster as we know kids today. I didn't turn professional until I was twenty-six years old, after a stint in the Coast Guard.

The course was to my liking. Except for the seventeenth, the par-fives

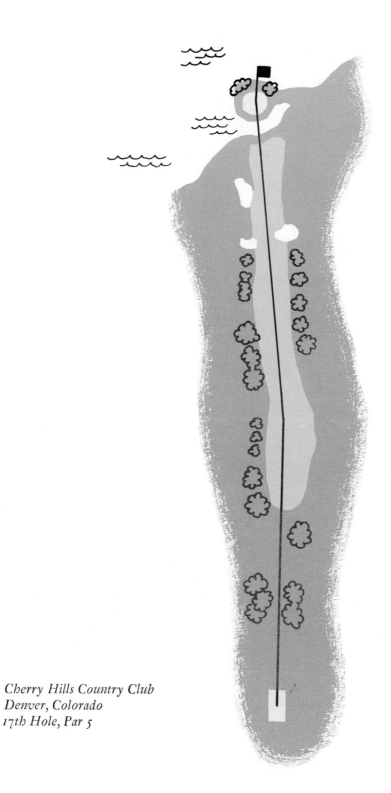

Cherry Hills Country Club
Denver, Colorado
17th Hole, Par 5

were reachable in two shots, the par-threes were difficult, and the par-fours were not routine. It was a championship course in every way. I felt I had a good chance.

In those days, the Open finished with thirty-six holes on Saturday. I remember making five birdies in the morning round and still finishing with a one-over-par seventy-two. Mike Souchak was running away with the tournament, but I had not conceded. At lunch I still thought I had a chance. I was the only one, even though history may well say that other people thought I did, too. You must remember that I was just one of a bunch of good young players trying to unseat Ben Hogan and Sam Snead—seemingly an impossible task.

I kept insisting that you could drive the first hole, and everybody said only an idiot would try. Well, I tried and made it. I think that one single shot opening the final round made me think that, perhaps, I was right and the rest were wrong.

At any rate, the key to the whole golf tournament was the seventeenth hole. It is a par-five that is short enough to be reached in two, but an island green forbids it. Hogan had bogeyed the hole and fallen out of the lead. I knew I had a good chance as I stood on the tee.

You must drive down a chute of trees, but the drive really isn't the important shot. The second shot is the key. You must lay up but get as close to the creek as possible. It is a demanding wedge shot, and it is important to be able to see all of the green. I got by the hole with a par and felt then that I had won, even though I had a tough finishing hole left to play.

I asked a long-time friend, Dow Finsterwald, to come back to Cherry Hills and relive my youth with me. Finsty, incidentally, was very much in contention back there in 1960. He scored a two-over-par seventy-three and was one of the guys I passed on the way to the Open title.

Finsty was a remarkable player in his younger days. He once finished in the money seventy-two straight times and almost became the only player to win the PGA title at match play and stroke play in consecutive years. He lost to Lionel Hebert at Miami Valley in Dayton in 1957 in the finals at match play and won the title the next year at Llanerch when it was turned to stroke play.

Normally, I favor par-five holes that give you a chance to go for the green in two. It makes the game more exciting when there is a risk involved. As I said before, you possibly could reach this green in two, but I don't think there is any way you could keep the ball on it and out of the water behind it.

Scenic view of hole.

Dow Finsterwald tees off.

This hole is a great hole simply because you have to play two good shots to get in position to play the third. Dow and I both drove well and played our second shots so that we were close enough for tight wedge shots. We both wedged within fifteen feet and took pars.

I couldn't help but think how easy the game is when the pressure is off and you are just going along hitting the ball. I can't imagine what it is like not to feel the charge when the bell rings. Everything changes, including your thinking. If things are working well, you think soundly. If things are wrong, you think poorly.

A low handicapper is in more trouble on this hole than most others. He would be wise to take a long iron off the tee, one that he feels he can control, rather than bust the driver. The green cannot be reached in two, and our low handicapper has to be a little wild off the tee at times. Otherwise he wouldn't have a handicap. A wild shot off that tee means trees and trouble.

The second shot, too, should be a controlled iron, and then all that is left is 100 to 120 yards. That way he insures that he can go for the green with his third shot. This sets up a possible birdie or a pretty sure par.

The middle handicapper can be in trouble here because accuracy is the name of the game, and our middle man is not as accurate as most. If he slices, there isn't enough room in the fairway to handle the full banana ball. If he

Arnold Palmer pitches across water to green.

Aerial view showing fairway back toward tee.

pulls the tee shot, good-bye. Perhaps our middle man should hit his three-wood twice, hoping to stay in the fairway, then lay up with his third, since the chances of holding the green with another wood or a long iron are quite slim.

Then, with wedge in hand, our middle man is back where he can do something. A wedge shot and either one or two putts and he has a very respectable score on the hole.

The high man, alas, will have to let a lot of people play through as he struggles along looking for his ball, either in the woods or in the water. The hole was not designed for him (no holes are, really), but he probably should not even contest this one. It is too tough for him. If he does, I'm afraid he is destined to mark his scorecard in double figures.

A lot has happened to me since 1960, but I still often think about Cherry Hills. I am a lifelong member there and return as often as I can. After all, how many times does a guy win his first Open championship?

Olympic Club

SAN FRANCISCO, CALIFORNIA

LAKE COURSE, 16th HOLE, 604 YARDS, PAR 5

It was at the Olympic Club on San Francisco's south shoreline on a hot summer day in 1966 that I dreamed of breaking Ben Hogan's U. S. Open record. While I was dreaming, Bill Casper kept playing golf and made up a seven-shot deficit on the final nine holes to tie me for the Open championship after four rounds. He won the playoff the next day, turning my dream into a nightmare.

Olympic was a disaster area for Ben Hogan, too. Hogan seemingly had his fifth U. S. Open championship in his pocket when a golfer of little national repute played the round of a lifetime, caught Hogan, and beat him in a playoff. His name was Jack Fleck.

The mighty, curving sixteenth hole, at 604 yards the longest on the course, was where the disastrous turns of fortune for me reached their peak. Throughout the championship, I had driven magnificently long and straight, but I hooked into the heavy rough at the sixteenth. That wasn't so bad, but I tried to hit a long iron out of the rough and muffed it, winding up with a bogey. My lead had shrunk from seven to one. Few people remember that I had to sink a breaking downhill three-footer at the eighteenth just to tie Casper and get in the playoff. I also had to get down in two shots from a greenside trap at the sixteenth. Actually, I made a good bogey.

177

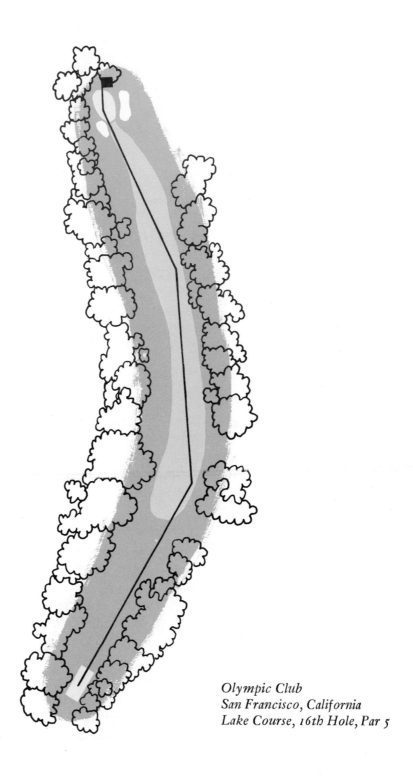

Olympic Club
San Francisco, California
Lake Course, 16th Hole, Par 5

Fleck, on the other hand, having birdied the fifteenth in his brilliant round eleven years earlier, got ready to halt Hogan's rise above everybody else in Open history, taking his place in golfing lore by saving par from the rough on sixteen.

If I were ever going to really believe that a tournament had a little bit of a jinx on me, one in which I've played pretty well through the years, it would have to be the Open. People ask me about the jinx of the PGA, which I have never won, yet I recall the things that have happened to me in the Open more readily.

Losing the playoff at Olympic to Casper after blowing that big lead; Oakmont, where I three-putted eleven times and lost to Jack Nicklaus; Brookline, where Julius Boros beat me in yet another playoff. I could add Pebble Beach, where I missed that short putt at the sixty-ninth hole when I could have taken the lead, and again in 1973, where Johnny Miller scored a sixty-three in the last round and I missed a four-footer at eleven to keep abreast.

Fleck played a head-to-head match with Hogan's score at Olympic in 1955. Fleck was at the first tee—he was the next-to-last starter in the field that day—as Hogan was finishing his final round. Jack knew what was demanded of him, scored sixty-seven, and forced the playoff. Then he continued his remarkable play, scoring sixty-nine to Hogan's seventy-two in the playoff.

The sixteenth hole traces a long, sweeping dogleg from right to left over its 604 yards. It is necessary to keep the second shot in the right side of the fairway to avoid a large tree that juts into the fairway at the left. Two woods usually leave a six- or seven-iron approach to a large, tricky green that is fronted on both sides by traps.

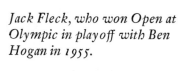
Jack Fleck, who won Open at Olympic in playoff with Ben Hogan in 1955.

I lost two shots of my seven-shot lead at the sixteenth when I made that bogey and Casper birdied. Oddly enough, I had been fading the ball slightly all week, but went back to my normal right-to-left shot that day and hit the ball into the rough.

Jack Fleck agreed to come back to the scene of his greatest triumph and play the hole with me. Fleck, fifty-one years old, has been in club work in the Midwest and California since the early 1960s. He is a native of Bettendorf, Iowa, and was almost a total unknown when he defeated Hogan. Oddly, his two other tour victories also were achieved in the West and in playoffs. He made a strong bid to win another Open in 1960 at Cherry Hills.

The Open really had an influence on Fleck's life. He is not an outgoing man and was not used to public speaking. When you are the Open champion, many extra activities are involved. Jack was not ready for it, he admits himself, and, for two years after his Open victory, he couldn't get untracked.

The day we played, the weather was perfect in San Francisco. Both Jack and I hit good drives and positioned our second shots so that we both used seven-irons to the green. We two-putted for pars and left feeling the influence that the sixteenth hole had had on our lives.

Our low handicapper has to be careful on this hole, as he needs the length to get close enough to hit a high iron but cannot be wild with either his tee shot or fairway wood. Anything off line and he is in bogey territory. However, the low handicapper has the length to reach the green in three shots, and four should be his limit, giving him either one or two putts for a par.

Our medium handicapper has a problem. The hole is probably too long for him to reach with three woods, and he will more likely have to hit four shots to get home—that is, if he keeps the ball in the fairway, a large order for our slice specialist. I would say seven would be a good score for our medium player. Either his drive or one of the other fairway shots will probably stray into the rough, necessitating an iron shot along the way. So if he gets on the green in five, he has done well, and we give him two putts for a seven. If he one-putts for a six, that is his par.

Our high handicapper may never finish this hole if he doesn't start early in the morning. He could run out of daylight. Bumping along a hole more than six hundred yards long will test his patience. However, if he plays carefully and doesn't try to slug the ball, he could get home in six or seven and avoid double figures.

When you consider that the world's greatest players struggle for a par-five at the sixteenth, you realize the dilemma confronting our high man.

Aerial view of picturesque clubhouse, showing 18th green in front.

The 1955 Open championship also produced a laughable sidelight. Bob Drum, my old newspaperman friend who worked with me on this book, had been in San Francisco for a week with two of his pals—Howard Gill, publisher of *Golf Digest*, and Dan Jenkins, now of *Sports Illustrated*. They had been having a big time doing the town and each night reporting home that they were enjoying the city.

On the telecast the final day, Gene Sarazen announced as Ben Hogan walked off the green that "Hogan has just become the first man to win five U. S. Open championships." The television then went off the air while Fleck was still playing the back nine. Of course, he eventually tied Hogan to force the playoff.

Drum called home that night and the conversation went something like this:

DRUM: "I have to stay here another day because of a playoff."

WIFE: "What playoff? Hogan won. I heard the TV announcer say so. Don't give me any of that malarkey."

DRUM: "Honest, there's a playoff. I wouldn't kid you."

WIFE: "Who is in this phantom playoff?"

Aerial view of approach to 16th green.

DRUM: "A guy named Jack Fleck."

WIFE: "Fleck? You big bum, you would make up a name like that. I thought you might come up with another of your fictitious names like Baxter Blodgett."

TELEPHONE: CLICK!!

Imagine her surprise when she read the newspaper the next day.

Scenic view of 16th green.

Dunes Golf and Beach Club

MYRTLE BEACH, SOUTH CAROLINA

18th HOLE, 540 YARDS, PAR 5

The best known of the plethora of fine courses at South Carolina's coastal golfing resort of Myrtle Beach is the Dunes Golf and Beach Club. The Dunes, opened back in the 1950s when Myrtle Beach's boom began, has hosted many important amateur championships since then and was the scene of Murle Lindstrom Breer's victory in the 1962 U. S. Women's Open championship. Since those days, more than twenty fine courses have been constructed in the area, including the seventy-two-hole Myrtle Beach National layout, for which I served as design consultant. These and other courses at Myrtle Beach may well challenge the Dunes' reputation as they become time- and competition-tested.

The most famous hole at the Dunes is the monstrous, par-five thirteenth, a hole shaped like a boomerang around a lake. However, the eighteenth hole has seen more heartbreak and presents a challenge that I like to face—whether to go for the green with the second shot or play safe.

Even from the back tee, with a solid, properly directed drive, I can reach the green in two strokes. However, the second shot is blind into a green that slopes toward you with woods on the right, a trap at the left front, a bush-covered hillock to the left and rear and, most dangerously, a pond in the front.

183

Annually, the Golf Writers' Association of America, people who for the most part write about golf better than they play it, gather in Myrtle Beach to play their annual golf (?) tournament at the Dunes.

One year, a friend of mine, Dudley (Waxo) Green of the Nashville *Banner*, needed an eight on the eighteenth to tie for the net title. He made twelve. Des Sullivan, a long-time writer and player who has always been a great chipper, took four from the edge another year, so shaken was he after putting his third in the water. Yet Des tied Dan Jenkins of *Sports Illustrated* and won the playoff.

At the other end of the spectrum, Bill Brendle of CBS once reached the eighteenth needing a twelve to tie John Husar of the Chicago *Tribune* and avoid posting the highest score of the day. Bill sank a ten-foot putt for the needed twelve and a 143.

A low handicapper should have little trouble making a par here unless he hits a bad tee shot or takes a poor-percentage gamble with his second shot. Any kind of a tee shot and he can reach the green with a wood or less, and chances for a birdie are high.

Our middle handicapper lays up and then just needs a pitch over the water, a relatively easy shot if the right club is chosen for the lay-up and the ball is kept away from the tree-lined edges of the fairway. Sometimes, as in Waxo Green's case, the shot doesn't come off. The middle man should make par.

Our high handicapper, even with grounders, can get to the edge of the pond in four shots. Now he needs to get over the water and into the hole, always a problem. He's a sure-fire candidate for double figures on this finishing hole.

Riviera Country Club

LOS ANGELES, CALIFORNIA

1st HOLE, 508 YARDS, PAR 5

The first at Riviera can be a very rewarding hole or an extremely disappointing one. It is short enough to be reached in two strokes, but is also divided by a gully which, on most occasions, has water in it.

The gully does not come into play when the wind is against you but can be reached from the tee when the weather is calm or the wind is in your favor.

George Low, who may have been around that long, recalls George Von Elm, not one of the longer hitters, bouncing the ball across the gully and having a short iron to the green one day back in the Depression.

It's a nervous driving hole because the left is out of bounds. Many a golfer has set up wrong and hit a hook into somebody's yard.

Our low handicapper is a cinch to hit one out of bounds every now and then since he wants to crush the ball and get home in two. Even when he does crush it in the right direction, the second shot is a lot more difficult than it looks. A well-bunkered green demands a well-aimed long iron or wood. If he plays within himself and doesn't try to outhit the long hitters, our low man should make an easy par and have a shot at a birdie.

Our middle man has his best chance for a birdie here. Two wood shots will put him well beyond the gulch and set up a short shot to get close to the pin. Ordinarily, middle men are good chippers and putters, so he has an easy par and a possible birdie.

Our high handicapper is not so fortunate. His third shot may not be long enough to clear the creek, so he should lay up. Then two or three more shots to the green and two putts. Seven or eight. Old high must be getting tired by now. That's what he gets for not taking some lessons.

Waverly Country Club

PORTLAND, OREGON

18th HOLE, 580 YARDS, PAR 5

Among the fine young players on the tour is Lanny Wadkins, a graduate of my alma mater, Wake Forest, and a recipient of the Buddy Worsham golf scholarship there, I'm proud to add.

Lanny is considered a brash young man, but I prefer to think that he is self-confident and straightforward. Some of the things he says are lost in translation. I like him.

When he won the U. S. Amateur championship at the Waverly Country Club in Portland, Oregon, he was five strokes behind Tom Kite coming to the eighteenth hole in the third round. Kite, another fine young pro, was playing one group behind Wadkins and watched Lanny hole an eighty-yard wedge shot for an eagle three. Kite then bogeyed the hole, and Lanny had made up three shots.

The next day Wadkins birdied two and three to get even and came to the eighteenth hole needing a birdie to win. He holed a twenty-footer for the four and won the championship by one stroke.

The eighteenth is a long par-five that cannot be reached in two shots. A river flows along the right side of the fairway, in sight all the way. This tends to make you favor the left toward a range of trees.

Two good wood shots and a short pitch to the green usually get you in position for a birdie try. However, the ball must be kept on line and away from the water.

Our low handicapper should have a picnic with this hole, since he rarely hits the ball right, and there is room on the left. I have him putting for a birdie most of the time.

Our middle handicapper is in trouble here. The usual slice will give the ball a bath at least once on this hole, since he must hit three wood shots to get home. Three wood shots, even without going in the water, a chip, and two putts for a six.

Our high handicapper will just keep swinging away and should get home in seven or eight shots. He needs a one-putter to escape double figures.

La Costa Country Club

CARLSBAD, CALIFORNIA

17th HOLE, 571 YARDS, PAR 5

La Costa Country Club, a plush resort that materialized in the early 1960s pretty much in the middle of nowhere, just inland along the Southern California coast north of San Diego, has been identified with a wide variety of golf tournaments in its relatively brief existence. However, it is now readily recognized as the home of the unique Tournament of Champions, which it has hosted since the tournament was moved from Las Vegas, its original home, in 1969.

Many great players have won the Tournament of Champions, both during its sixteen years in Las Vegas and since it has been at La Costa. I have been fortunate enough to have won it three times (1962, 1965 and 1966) and had one of the more frustrating rounds of my career when I tried for a fourth win in 1967. I trailed Frank Beard by six shots going into the final round, played at the Stardust Country Club that year, and got off to a great start—birdie-eagle-birdie on the first three holes. I shot twenty-nine on the front side and figured I was going to make it three in a row.

On the back nine, though, I four-putted one green, missed a sixteen-incher at another, and watched as Beard birdied the final hole to beat me by a shot. That's why golf is a great game: You get going and then you get trapped. It keeps you on your toes all the time.

But that's getting away from the course I started talking about and the good par-five seventeenth, a hole that will yield birdies, but not easily. Traps and heavy rough protect the left side of the fairway much of the way from tee to green. A lake on the right begins about 275 yards out and runs the rest of the way to and beside the green. The water does not present much of a risk off the tee, but will grab second and third shots that drift ever so slightly to the right. The approach is particularly dangerous when the pin is cut to the right on the big green or close behind the big trap in front. The prevailing wind is in your face on this hole, making it almost impossible to reach the green in two. The earlier you play the better, because the wind gets stronger in the afternoon.

From this description you can see that it is a tough hole for all of our levels of players but particularly hazardous for our slice-inclined middle handicapper. It will be bogeys or worse for just about all of them.

The first year we played at La Costa, I was tied for the lead after nine holes of the third round. I promptly made seven at ten, but still came to seventeen with a chance to win. I hit my second shot in the water, took another seven, and wound up third as Gary Player won it. I guess I still thought the tournament was in Vegas, where seven is a lucky number.

In 1972, Bobby Mitchell beat Jack Nicklaus in a playoff, despite an unnerving experience at the seventeenth in the final round. After playing three outstanding pressure shots there, Bobby muffed a two-foot birdie putt that ultimately cost him victory in seventy-two holes. With that miss so fresh in his mind, Bobby figured to have little chance against Nicklaus in the playoff. But instead, Bobby holed a twenty-footer on the first extra hole for the victory and celebrated by going out and buying a hairpiece. When Jack saw Bobby a few weeks later with the new store hair, Jack remarked:

"I knew it was a good win for you, Bobby, but how did it grow hair on your head?"

Arizona Country Club

18th HOLE, 528 YARDS, PAR 5

In some tournaments, birdies and eagles are commonplace. Purists object to this, but it is hard to argue with the excitement that they generate. Watching travail all day long is not what most spectators prefer at a tournament. They experience enough anguish with their own games and would rather watch the stars excel.

That is precisely why I chose the finishing hole at Arizona Country Club. It is admittedly not an overly strong par-five, but it has produced some great finishes. The Phoenix Open, which is played at Arizona Country Club every other year, produces some of the most spectacular scoring on the tour. Somebody always seems to shoot a sixty-one or sixty-two in the tournament. In the early 1970s Johnny Miller and Homero Blancas did it.

The eighteenth is a short par-five at 528 yards and within iron range of most of the tour players on their second shots. Trees and bushes guard both sides of a narrow fairway, and the drive must be placed well before you can try to get home in two.

This hole not only produces many thrilling shots but also was the site of an incident that apparently led to an important change in the rules of golf. In 1963, the year I won and Gary Player finished second, Gary was playing with Don January and was several holes ahead of me. In the final round,

Player had his ball within eight feet of the hole and was waiting to putt for a birdie.

January putted from farther away. The ball rolled right to the lip of the cup, looked in, but did not fall. Don waited a long time, hoping for it to drop, contending the ball appeared to be moving and, under the rules then, he would be penalized for hitting a moving ball. He eventually tapped in.

The long wait upset Gary. He missed his putt and lost by a stroke to me. Luckily I birdied that hole for the victory, which I remember well because it was my third straight Phoenix Open title.

At the start of the next season, the USGA changed the rule covering situations in which a ball is overhanging the hole, preventing a player from stalling more than "a few seconds."

Arizona's eighteenth should give our low handicapper the same shot at a birdie or eagle as we pros have unless his hooking tendencies tangle him up with bushes or trees. The dogleg right helps the middle handicapper in his quest for a closing par.

Even the high handicapper has a chance for a one-putt par if he can keep his bump-and-run shots in play. That par on the last hole will be just as exciting for him as are the pros' birdies and eagles to the Phoenix Open galleries.

NCR Country Club

DAYTON, OHIO

SOUTH COURSE,
6th HOLE, 548 YARDS, PAR 5

I played the sixth hole at the NCR Country Club only once, in the 1969 PGA championship in Dayton, Ohio, but I will remember it forever. It was on this hole that I thought my career might be finished.

To backtrack, I somehow injured my right hip at New Orleans in 1966 and had some trouble with it from time to time after that. It acted up again the day before the PGA at Dayton, and I was apprehensive when I started the round. You see, I rely so much on a strong right side to get my power.

I won't blame it all on the aching hip, but I started the tournament disastrously by bogeying the first three holes, then never touched the cup with a par putt from eighteen inches at the fourth.

I wasn't about to give up, though, and felt I could get a stroke or two back at that long, par-five sixth hole when I managed to get off a good drive. This left me with a chance to get home in two, but it would take a big shot. A valley of rough lies between that part of the fairway and the green, set into the opposite hillside. The late Dick Wilson, when he designed the course for the huge National Cash Register Corporation in 1954, virtually surrounded the green with traps. It's out of bounds at the tree line to the left.

I wanted that eagle chance, so I went all out with a one-iron shot—and the hip really caught me. It was a struggle just to finish the round in eighty-two strokes, and I withdrew the next morning and went home for treatment. Fortunately, the hip responded to treatment, relieving my fears of an early forced retirement from the game I love.

Still, it was a great setback for me, as I had looked forward eagerly to playing the NCR course and thought I would be a contender for that one major title I had not yet collared. I have always been rather partial to Dick Wilson courses—he laid out two that are very close to me, Laurel Valley at home and my Bay Hill course at Orlando—and usually play them well.

Unless he gets quite wild, the low handicapper we have talked about should be able to cope with NCR's sixth. Pars and occasional birdies. The middle handicapper ought to get on the green in four occasionally, but you know the high handicapper will be spending time in that ravine in front of the green.

Atlanta Country Club

ATLANTA, GEORGIA

18th HOLE, 512 YARDS, PAR 5

Atlanta Country Club's par-five eighteenth is another one of those do-or-don't holes. You can play it safe, but that is not the way to win unless, of course, you have a three- or four-shot lead in the final round and are coasting.

This 512-yard hole demands two tremendous shots to reach the green in two. However, it is done and done often when the drive is well placed and well hit.

The first year the Atlanta Classic was played on the course, Jack Nicklaus made eight on the hole, an exceptional occurrence.

A lake guards the entire left side of the fairway, which circles around the water to the right. You tee off on a dam, go over or around one lake, and then have to cross another to reach the green. The water comes right up to the front edge of a green that slopes toward it. Traps right and left add to the demand for accuracy of any bid to hit the green in two from that long range.

The natural urge of the low handicapper to go for it will cost him strokes most of the time. The lake shouldn't cause too many problems for the middle and the high handicapper, just force them away from it at the cost of strokes because of the roundabout route.

When Nicklaus made his eight, he dumped his tee shot into the edge of the lake and chipped out. He then put his third shot in the lake, dropped, and pitched into the green. Naturally, like all of us after that kind of trouble, he three-putted.

Tommy Aaron, who later won the Masters, captured his first official PGA tournament in the 1970 Atlanta Classic by, of all things, playing safe at the final hole.

Aaron steered clear of the water on both of his first two shots, pitched on the green, and two-putted for a par. Then he stood behind the green to watch his two main adversaries, Gary Player and Tom Weiskopf, try to beat him.

Weiskopf hooked his tee shot into the water to eliminate himself, and Player, trying for the win, dumped his second shot in the second lake. Aaron finally had the title that had eluded him for so long—and in his home state, yet.

Bermuda Dunes Country Club

BERMUDA DUNES, CALIFORNIA

18th HOLE, 520 YARDS, PAR 5

It would be hard for me to come up with anything uncomplimentary to say about Palm Springs and its California desert surroundings. My golf seems to flourish in that desert setting. I have won five Bob Hope Desert Classics in the Palm Springs area, more victories than I have in any other tournament. Bermuda Dunes and its eighteenth hole have to be my favorites of the Classic courses there because I have completed four of my winning efforts at the eighteenth there or went on to successful playoffs from there.

The eighteenth at Bermuda Dunes is a par-five that can be reached in two strokes. However, in order to accomplish this feat, a pond that guards the green in front and around the right side must be taken into consideration.

Usually I try to go for the green in two, but it depends on the drive. It has to be a good one to give you a chance to reach the putting surface. It must be long and straight because of palm trees along the right side of the fairway short of the water and heavy rough; trees and out of bounds along the left side. If the second shot is a "no go" to the green, it is played straight down the fairway to the opening to the green, which sits off to the right behind the pond. From the air, the hole resembles a giant golf club.

In 1973 I was starting to doubt whether I would ever be a contender again. I had not won for more than a year, and everything seemed to be going wrong. But the desert elixir worked again. I was in the battle from the second day on. On the fifth day, I went at it head to head with Jack Nicklaus.

Going to that final hole at Bermuda Dunes, I had a two-stroke lead. Jack reached the green in two and had an eagle putt to try from about thirty feet. I pitched up about seven feet from the hole in three and watched with, quite frankly, little apprehension as Jack just missed. I was convinced that I was going to make my putt whether or not Jack made his. I rolled it in to win by two. It was a great feeling, as I think was reflected by news pictures snapped at that moment.

My first win at Bermuda Dunes was in 1962, and the other two were in playoffs against Deane Beman in 1968 and Ray Floyd in 1971, which, incidentally, also broke a long victory drought. I lost another Bob Hope Classic playoff—to Doug Sanders in 1966. Doug was seven under on the final nine at Indian Wells and birdied the first playoff hole. Too bad it wasn't at Bermuda Dunes. I might have had another win.

Canterbury Golf Club

CLEVELAND, OHIO

16th HOLE, 605 YARDS, PAR 5

Cleveland became my second home in the early 1950s while I was in the Coast Guard. I played a lot of amateur golf while I was in Cleveland in the Coast Guard and afterward when I worked there in a sales position. I was living there when I won both the Ohio and the National Amateur championships in 1954.

The Cleveland area abounds with fine golf courses, none finer than Canterbury, which has hosted its share of national championships. Lawson Little won the Open there in 1940 to become only the sixth man in history to have won both the U. S. Amateur and the U. S. Open. Since then, Gene Littler, Jack Nicklaus, and I have joined that group.

Little's playoff victory over Gene Sarazen at Canterbury is memorable more for what happened to Ed (Porky) Oliver than the fact that Lawson won. Oliver was among six players who teed off before their starting times. The weather bureau was predicting thunderstorms, and two threesomes, finding the first tee open and untended for the final afternoon round and anxious to get in as many holes as possible before the bad weather hit, went out ahead of schedule. All of them—Claude Harmon, Ky Laffoon, Johnny Bulla, Duke Gibson, Dutch Harrison, and Oliver—were notified while on the course that they were disqualified. But they played the full eighteen holes anyway. The rollicking, popular Porky finished with a 287, the score that put Little and Sarazen into the playoff.

At 605 yards, the sixteenth at Canterbury is a brute of a par-five hole, not one that has the second-shot challenge, other than to keep the ball in play for a relatively short third shot to the green. The tee shot is hit out of a chute onto a very uneven fairway, which falls away to the right. Trees line the entire right side from the landing area to the green, and there are patches of trees down the left side as well. The fairway rises to a plateau, which is the best target for the second shot, since the fairway dips again in front of the green. Trees pinch in from both sides at that plateau, making the second shot a critical one. The rather small green has traps left and rear—and more trees.

The sixteenth is part of the home stretch at Canterbury, where nearly all of the major championships played there have been decided. Byron Nelson "lost" an Open in that stretch in 1946. He parred the sixteenth but three-putted the par-three seventeenth and double-bogeyed the eighteenth to fall into a tie with Lloyd Mangrum and Vic Ghezzi. Mangrum won the subsequent playoff.

Jack Nicklaus experienced no difficulties but made no birdies at the sixteenth when he won his third PGA championship, at Canterbury, in 1973.

Rio Pinar Country Club

ORLANDO, FLORIDA

15th HOLE, 510 YARDS, PAR 5

Rio Pinar has enjoyed a national reputation for many years now through its association with professional golf—in the late 1950s as the scene of several matches in a television series, and since 1966 as the host of the Florida Citrus Open on our winter tour.

Among the interesting holes on this Orlando course is the par-five fifteenth. Architect Mark Mahannah must have had Augusta National and its thirteenth hole in mind when he designed the fifteenth at Rio Pinar (recall my earlier description of Augusta's thirteenth). The dogleg of the fifteenth swings right instead of left, but the hole presents the same sort of challenge as at Augusta—a long second shot to a slightly elevated green that can be reached in two but with a creek angling across the fairway in front of it, though not as close to the putting surface as at Augusta. The creek runs along the left side beyond a bunker, and a large trap protects the right side of the green.

The Citrus Open is a regular stop for me, since Orlando is my favorite area of Florida. I have always liked the weather and the people in Orlando and, as I point out elsewhere in the book, I am the president and major owner of another Orlando club, Bay Hill, where I maintain my winter home.

I have had varying success in the Citrus Open, including winning the championship in 1971, and have shot some fine scores at Rio Pinar, usually with the help of birdies or eagles at the fifteenth. In 1970, I shot sixty-fours in the first and third rounds, yet lost by a stroke to Bob Lunn. I recall an earlier year in which I had a good shot at winning until the fifteenth hole grabbed me when I went for the green from marginal range and caught the water.

The year I won I opened with a sixty-six off five consecutive birdies in the middle of the round, and it came down to a duel for the title with Julius Boros, with whom I had shared the lead after fifty-four holes. Boros birdied the fifteenth in that final round to cut my lead to a single stroke, but I mustered a birdie myself at the seventeenth and beat him by a shot with an eighteen-under-par 270.

The fifteenth dictates a lay-up second shot for all except the best of the low handicappers, who, incidentally, must guard against driving the ball through the fairway into the pines. A small patch of trees and a pond at the dogleg on the right side present problems for the middle and the high handicappers, who will be taking sixes, sevens, and eights in most of their rounds.

The Citrus Open is one of the few remaining bastions of the "community effort" tournament. Most tournaments today rely heavily on one big sponsor for a large amount of the financing, but in Orlando many of the businesses in the community pitch in to make the tournament a success. This is another reason why I enjoy playing there.

Upper Montclair Country Club

CLIFTON, NEW JERSEY

11th HOLE, 530 YARDS, PAR 5

Upper Montclair Country Club holds the distinction, for what it's worth, of being the place where golf's first three-hundred-thousand-dollar tournament was played. The only Dow Jones Open ever staged was held at Upper Montclair in 1970 and, typically, Bobby Nichols picked up the sixty-thousand-dollar first-place check.

Nichols, who has done this elsewhere in big-money events, came to the last hole facing an eighteen-foot putt for a birdie and a win, two putts for a tie with Labron Harris. Bobby sank it, bringing everybody back in from the fifteenth hole, where they had gone, expecting a playoff.

Upper Montclair also hosted the first Thunderbird Classic in 1962, when Gene Littler took the twenty-five-thousand-dollar first prize, then the biggest in golf since George May's fifty-thousand-dollar awards to the winners of the World at Tam O'Shanter in Chicago. I won my second Thunderbird Classic in 1967, and that paid thirty thousand dollars. They wrote big checks at Upper Montclair.

Birdies on the par-five eighteenth actually brought victories to Nichols and me, but I admire more the par-five eleventh, a 530-yard hole that offers the same challenge as the two par-fives on the back nine of Augusta National —a chance to reach the green in two if you gamble to cross water. However, this requires a long, left-to-right tee shot safely into the tree-lined fairway.

For most players, the hole plays with a tee shot, a midiron short of the fifty-foot-wide pond, and a wedge to the green. That, of course, is providing these less-skilled players keep the ball out of the rough and the trees.

Interestingly, Nichols got the stroke he needed to edge Labron Harris in 1970 by knocking his third shot at the eleventh hole out of the trees and onto the green, then holing the birdie putt. Bobby is a man after my own heart—undaunted when he puts his ball into trouble, figuring, as I do, that there has to be a way out.

Broadmoor Golf Club

COLORADO SPRINGS, COLORADO

EAST COURSE, 18th HOLE, 460 YARDS, PAR 5

Most people go to the Broadmoor for the fantastic Rocky Mountain scenery of Colorado Springs and golf (not necessarily in that order), but my most recent visits there have not been to play but rather in connection with a new eighteen-hole course I and my architect associate, Ed Seay, laid out for the Broadmoor, which has magnificent grounds for golf. Colorado's long winters constitute a drawback, but the snow certainly helps to grow grass. The Broadmoor courses have some of the finest fairways and greens I have ever seen.

The Broadmoor already had thirty-six holes, and the U. S. Amateur championship has been contested on both courses. Bob Dickson won there in 1967, beating Vinnie Giles on the final hole on the West Course.

But the hole we are concerned about is the eighteenth on the East Course, where Jack Nicklaus met Charley Coe in the finals of the U. S. Amateur championship in 1959.

It is a 460-yard par-five, with a slight dogleg to the left, and a raised green. It is a great spectator hole, as an eagle is not out of the question, yet if you miss the green, a bogey is almost a certainty.

Coming to this hole even, Nicklaus hit a gorgeous shot just below the pin about ten feet from the hole. He looked like a sure winner when Coe hit his shot right over the flag. It came to rest on a downslope some thirty yards from the stick.

However, Coe hit one of the great chip shots of all time, almost holing out for his four. Nicklaus promptly knocked in his putt for a three and claimed the championship, his first of two before turning pro in late 1961.

Of course, I have fond memories of Colorado, too. Denver is just up the road a piece from the Broadmoor, and Denver is where I won my Open championship, at Cherry Hills.

Two days before the Open, Pat McDonough, an old Pittsburgh friend of mine who was an eight handicapper at the time, was playing a casual round at the Broadmoor with Chi Chi Rodriguez. Chi Chi was working there for Ed Dudley, who had been his mentor and close friend in Puerto Rico.

When they reached the eighteenth (not the fifteenth hole), Chi Chi was one down. But he put his wood second shot on the green ten feet from the hole, putting for an eagle. Pat reached the fringe in three, holed his chip shot, had a stroke coming with his handicap, and so made a net three. Even though Chi Chi sank his putt, Pat won the bet.

"How about that," Chi Chi complained mildly. "I make eagle on a hole and lose it to an old bald-headed man."